BREAKING THE CODE

The Mysteries of Modern Management *Unlocked*

Based on the works of L. Ron Hubbard

Published by RAVENWOOD MANAGEMENT GROUP
1717 E. Vista Chino, Suite A7, PMB 127, Palm Springs, California 92262
E-mail: info@rmgpubs.com   Phone: (760) 416-1141
Website: www.BreakingTheCodeBook.com

Copyright © 2009, 2011 by Ravenwood Management Group

All rights reserved. No part of this publication may be reproduced, stored in a retrieval system or transmitted in any form or by any means, electronic, mechanical, photocopying, recording or otherwise, without the express written permission of the copyright owner.

Grateful acknowledgment is made to L. Ron Hubbard Library for permission to reproduce selections from the copyrighted works of L. Ron Hubbard.

HUBBARD is a trademark and is used pursuant to a licensing agreement.

Third Edition   I/A No. 99071402RB

Printed in the United States of America

23 22 21 20 19 18 17   16 15 14 13 12 11 10 9 8

ISBN 978-0-9657874-3-7

IMPORTANT NOTE

BREAKING THE CODE: THE MYSTERIES OF MODERN MANAGEMENT UNLOCKED contains quotations from more than a dozen books and nearly 100 articles written by L. Ron Hubbard. The initial publication dates span a period of 35 years. Mr. Hubbard developed his administrative technology[1] in the course of running his own enterprises and foundations. With its use, he achieved rapid and stable international expansion, which he maintained throughout his life.

This book is designed specifically for ease of application in any type of organization.[2] Wherever possible, quotations from Mr. Hubbard's books and articles are reprinted verbatim. In some instances, quotations from multiple sources that cover the same topic have been merged to provide the reader with continuity of material. Also, references to job titles and terms that could only apply to Mr. Hubbard's organizations have been deleted and, where appropriate, replaced with job titles and terms routinely encountered in the workplace. However, unusual terms or expressions that could apply to any business, but might not be readily understood by the reader, remain unchanged and are defined in this book.

Quotations that have been edited or merged as described above are not annotated as such where they occur in this book, because those annotations would be both distracting to the reader and immaterial to the objective of Breaking The Code. However, the reader may be assured that, in all cases, Mr. Hubbard's original concepts remain unchanged.

In addition to the quotations from Mr. Hubbard's published works, Breaking The Code provides illustrations, examples and editorial comments to aid the reader in achieving full understanding of the concepts presented herein.

In order to clearly distinguish Mr. Hubbard's writings from examples and commentary provided by Ravenwood Management Group (RMG), we have printed the paragraphs that contain text that is mostly or entirely attributed to Mr. Hubbard (whether edited or directly quoted) in a different typeface from that used for examples and commentary.

> This typeface is used for text attributed to L. Ron Hubbard.
>
> This typeface is used for RMG's examples and editorial commentary.

WORDS

In reading this book, be very certain you never go past a word you do not fully understand. The only reason a person gives up a study[3] or becomes confused or unable to learn is because he or she has gone past a word that was not understood. The confusion or inability to grasp[4] or learn comes AFTER a word the person did not have defined and understood.

---

[1] **technology: 1.** the methods of application of an art or science as opposed to mere knowledge of the science or art itself. **2.** the whole body of the science. *Abbr.* **tech.**

[2] **organization:** a number of persons or groups having specific responsibilities and united for some purpose or work; a company.

[3] **study:** the pursuit of a particular branch of learning, science or art.

[4] **grasp:** to take hold of mentally; understand; comprehend.

If the material becomes confusing or you can't seem to grasp it, there will be a word just earlier that you have not understood. Don't go any further, but go back to BEFORE you got into trouble (i.e., got into a state of distress, annoyance or difficulty), find the misunderstood word and get it defined. It may not only be the new or unusual words you will have to look up. Some commonly used words can often be misdefined and so cause confusion.

There is a by-no-means-complete list of words that have to be fully defined and understood just to talk about organization[5] as a subject, and to intelligently and happily work in an organization. It is key vocabulary. Out of a full understanding of what is implied by each word, a brilliantly clean view is attained of the whole subject of organization as a crisp[6] usable activity. Glibness[7] won't do. For behind these words is the full structure of an activity that will survive and when the words aren't understood the rest can become foggy.

These basic words of organization, as well as words with special or unusual meanings or hard-to-find definitions, are defined in the glossary located in the back of the book, beginning on page 167. Words sometimes have several meanings. Each entry provides only the definition(s) of the word or phrase as it is used in this book. The glossary definitions are also footnoted on the pages where the defined words or phrases first appear in text. The glossary is not meant as a substitute for a dictionary. When reading this book, if you find any other words you do not know, look them up in a good dictionary.

---

[5] **organization:** the act of arranging personnel and materials in an orderly or systematic way. **Organization** consists of certain people doing certain jobs. The purpose of **organization** is to make planning become actuality.*

[6] **crisp:** distinct and clear, without ambiguity or distortion.

[7] **glib:** marked by disassociation of oneself from the materials one is studying. One doesn't associate the materials with anything; the words enter into one's consciousness on the surface only, with no awareness of the concepts they represent. The **glib student** can repeat what he's read or heard, but can't apply. —**glibly** (*adverb*) in a **glib** manner, —**glibness** (*noun*) the state of being **glib**.

INGREDIENTS OF SUCCESS

The conditions of success are few and easily stated.

Jobs are not held, consistently and in actuality, by flukes or fate or fortune. Those who depend upon luck generally experience bad luck. In today's society, we have come to a low level of the ability to work. Offices depend very often on no more than one or two people, and the additional personnel seem to add only complexity to the activities of the scene.

The ability to hold a job depends, in the main, *upon* ability. A vital part of success is the ability to handle and control not only one's tools of the trade, but the people with whom one is surrounded. In order to do this, one must be capable of a very high level of affinity, he must be able to tolerate many different realities (viewpoints) of his coworkers and he must, as well, be able to give and receive communication.

The ingredients of success are then, first, an ability to confront work with joy and not horror, a wish to do work for its own sake, not because one "has to have a paycheck." One must be able to work without driving oneself or experiencing deep depths of exhaustion. If one experiences these things, there is something wrong with him. There is some element in his environment that he *should be* controlling that he *isn't* controlling.

The ingredients of successful work are:

- Training and experience in the subject being addressed
- Good general intelligence and ability
- A capability of high affinity, a tolerance of reality (i.e., other people's viewpoints) and the ability to communicate and receive ideas.

Given these things, there is left only a slim chance of failure. One could have all the money in the world (whether acquired by birth, marriage or luck) and yet be unable to perform an hour's honest labor. Such a person would be a miserably unhappy one.

We know that people are not dispensable. It is a mechanism of old philosophies to tell people that if they think they are indispensable they should go down to the graveyard and take a look—those people were indispensable, too. This is the sheerest foolishness. If you really looked carefully in the graveyard, you would find the machinist who set the models going in yesteryear and without whom there would be no industry today. It is doubtful if such a feat is being performed just now. A workman is not *just* a workman. A laborer is not *just* a laborer. An office worker is not *just* an office worker. They are living, breathing, important pillars on which the entire structure of our civilization is erected. They are not cogs in a mighty machine. They are the machine itself.

IT IS TO THEM THAT THIS BOOK IS DEDICATED

CONTENTS

PREFACE ix

ACKNOWLEDGMENT xi

INCREASING UNDERSTANDING & DISCOVERING ONE'S POWER

Chapter 1: THE A-R-C TRIANGLE 1

Chapter 2: THE K-R-C TRIANGLE 9

BASIC ORGANIZATION

Chapter 3: UNDERSTANDING THE BASIC WORDS OF ORGANIZATION 15

Chapter 4: THE THEORY OF ORGANIZATION 17

Chapter 5: COMM LINES: DON'T JAM THEM 25

Chapter 6: WHAT AN EXECUTIVE WANTS ON HIS LINES 29

Chapter 7: YOUR JOB AND HOW TO KEEP IT 33

Chapter 8: ORGANIZATION AND MORALE 35

PRODUCTS AND EXCHANGE

Chapter 9: PRODUCTS AND SUBPRODUCTS 39

Chapter 10: EXCHANGE, COMPANY INCOME AND PAYROLL 45

THE USE OF STATISTICS

Chapter 11: THE CONDITIONS: Non-Existence and Above 51

Chapter 12: THE CONDITIONS: Below Non-Existence 65

Chapter 13: READING STATISTICS 69

Chapter 14: TARGETING OF STATISTICS AND QUOTAS 87

PLANNING

Chapter 15: BATTLE PLANS 97

Chapter 16: COORDINATION 101

Office Efficiency

Chapter 17: COMPANY COMMUNICATIONS SYSTEM 105

Chapter 18: COMPLETED STAFF WORK 111

Chapter 19: DEVELOPED TRAFFIC 115

Chapter 20: HOW TO HANDLE WORK 141

Ethics

Chapter 21: THE DESIGN OF ETHICS 145

Chapter 22: REWARDS AND PENALTIES 149

Chapter 23: ETHICS REPORTS 151

Successful Performance

Chapter 24: DUTIES OF AN EMPLOYEE 157

Chapter 25: PROVIDING GOOD SERVICE 159

Chapter 26: PROFESSIONALISM 161

Appendix

THE CONDITIONS FORMULAS 163

DEVELOPED TRAFFIC SUMMARY LIST 165

Glossary

..... 167

Index

..... 179

DISCLAIMER

In the English language, there is, unfortunately, no widely accepted gender-neutral pronoun to use when speaking about someone. When referring to an unspecified gender in writing, excessive use of "he/she" or "he or she" is clumsy and could be distracting to the reader. Use of "they" or "them" when referring to an individual is grammatically incorrect and, thus, could also be a distraction to the reader. Therefore, we have opted to use the conventional "he", "his" and "him" when referring to an individual whose gender is not otherwise specified. Such gender-specific references are not intended to limit the applicability or scope of the statement being made to one gender. "She" can readily be substituted for "he", and vice versa.

PREFACE

"Hat" is a term used to describe the write-ups,[8] checksheets[9] and packs[10] that outline the purposes, know-how[11] and duties[12] of a job position.[13]

Example: *Upon arrival at the office, John's boss gave him a binder containing the* **hat** *for his new job, with instructions to read it within a week.*

When one works in a company,[14] he must know how to function as a group member. The fundamental policies[15] and moral codes adopted for use by one's group could be called the "basic hat". It is necessary that, in addition to learning the specific duties and functions of the particular job for which one is trained, he must also learn his *basic hat* in order to be an effective, productive employee. The word *employee,* as used in this book, refers to any member of an organization, including executives, unless otherwise stated.

BREAKING THE CODE contains the essential elements of the *basic hat* — data that every employee needs to know in order to operate as part of a team — everything from the basics of organizing to the secrets of efficiency. The material contained in this book is presented in a logical sequence, beginning with the components of Understanding, which includes the subject of communication, as well as data on how to control one's environment. This is followed by the theory of how an organization works and the role an employee plays in it. We then cover the specific data on how one can monitor his personal production and what he can do to increase it. Then there are the tools to increase efficiency. The book concludes with data on how an employee can ensure his work environment is pleasant and his job is secure.

While one may achieve significant improvement in his job performance, measured in both productivity and efficiency, by simply reading this book and applying the technology contained herein, he could gain even greater insight and success by studying the material in the form of a supervised training course. Successful completion of the practical exercises contained in the course ensures that the student has fully understood and can thoroughly apply the materials he studied to his own job. Please contact the publisher for more information about online training.

It is our hope that you will assimilate the materials contained herein and use them to bring about greater efficiency and productivity on your job and in your company.

R. J. DiBerardo, Editor

---

[8] **write-up:** a written description of the operating procedures of a job position. This often includes a summary of the job functions, which is usually provided by the person who previously held the position.

[9] **checksheet:** a list of materials, often divided into sections, that give the theory and practical steps which, when completed, give one a study completion. The items are selected to add up to the required knowledge of the subject.

[10] **pack:** a collection of written materials which match a checksheet. A **pack** does not necessarily include a booklet or hardcover book that may be called for as part of a checksheet.

[11] **know-how:** knowledge of how to do something smoothly and efficiently; technical expertise, practical knowledge.

[12] **duties:** any actions, tasks, etc., required by or relating to one's occupation or position. [Example: *the* **duties** *of a secretary*]

[13] **position:** the name of the particular job one holds in any business which has its own distinguishing duties, responsibilities and products in relation to the other jobs in that business.

[14] **company:** a group of individuals, such as an association, corporation or partnership, associated for the purpose of carrying out, maintaining or performing a commercial or industrial enterprise.

[15] **policies:** the rules and administrative formulas by which members of an organization agree on action and conduct their affairs.

ACKNOWLEDGMENT

Hubbard® Administrative Technology

L. Ron Hubbard, American writer and philosopher, is well known as an explorer of ideas and technologies. He wrote more than 50 books on the subjects of philosophy, human relationships and the human mind, as well as business management.[16] He is one of the most acclaimed and widely read authors of all time, primarily because his works express a firsthand knowledge of the realities of life and what it really takes to accomplish something in it—knowledge gained not from standing on the sidelines but through lifelong experience with people from all walks of life.

When L. Ron Hubbard began to examine the problems of organization and management in the early 1950s, the serious lack of workable systems soon became obvious. This led him to begin an active search for basic laws governing the survival and expansion of all organizations and groups.

As a result of this search, he isolated for the first time the skills that a person needs to succeed. And with his keen understanding of life's fundamentals, he discovered and codified simple and practical steps through which one can sanely and easily create an expanding and enduring organization.

Whether your company or business is large or small, you will find that through the use of Hubbard Administrative Technology, you will have within your grasp the tools of limitless success and expansion.

Technology means the *methods of application* of the principles of something, as opposed to mere theoretical knowledge of the thing. This technology is for use. Its application brings results. If, as you study, you apply what you learn, this will become immediately evident. Today, this technology is broadly used around the world by organizations and businesses of all types and sizes—groups who now find themselves capable of rapid expansion and steady growth.

This textbook contains selections from Hubbard Administrative Technology that pertain to the fundamental duties and responsibilities of any member of an organization. With this technology, tremendous expansion can be obtained and sustained; goals can be achieved.

The success of any endeavor depends on many factors. Chief among these, of course, are having a clear purpose, the drive or desire to achieve one's goals and a willingness to improve and learn new things. Only you can get yourself moving on the road to success and if you possess the willingness to learn and actually apply the technology contained in this book, you will be well on your way!

---

[16] **management:** the planning of means to attain determined goals, assigning them to staff for execution, and proper coordination of activities within the group to attain maximum efficiency with minimal effort.

Increasing Understanding & Discovering One's Power

Chapter 1

THE A-R-C TRIANGLE

Cooperation is the act of working together to achieve a common goal. The word is derived from the Latin words **operare**, meaning *to work*, and **co**, meaning *together*. But there isn't any *together* where there is no understanding of what's occurring. So cooperation depends upon being able to see and grasp the scene. To *understand* is to have a clear and true idea or conception, or full and exact knowledge, of something. To *understand* implies the power to receive and register a clear and true impression. In an organization, as the understanding among coworkers increases, so will the level of cooperation. That helps to create a pleasant, harmonious workplace. So, it behooves every employee to learn the techniques of how to increase Understanding with others.

THE COMPONENTS OF UNDERSTANDING

The component parts of Understanding are: Affinity, Reality and Communication. One has to have some *affinity* for an object, some concept of its *reality*, and some *communication* with it, before he can understand it.

AFFINITY

Affinity, the first component of Understanding, is the feeling which exists between people or within a person. If affinity between two people is high we might use the word *love* as a synonym for this affinity. High affinity includes both *love* and *like*, and all feelings of goodwill and kinship. If the affinity is low we may use the word *hate* as a synonym for this affinity.

Affinity expresses the willingness to occupy the same place as the person or thing which is loved or liked. The reverse of it would be antipathy, *dislike* or rejection, which would be the unwillingness to occupy the same space as something or someone, or the unwillingness to approach something or someone.

There are no strings attached when affinity is given. To the receiver it carries no duties and no responsibilities. It is pure, easy and natural and flows out from you as easily as sunlight flows from the sun.

Affinity begets affinity. A person who is filled with the quality will automatically find people anywhere near him also beginning to be filled with affinity. It is a calming, warming, heartening influence on all who are capable of receiving and giving it.

REALITY

The next component of Understanding is reality. Reality is agreement. Agreement with what? Agreement with anything. It is surprising how much reality is dependent on an agreement between individuals that an object or an idea exists.

The old question, "Would the stone in the desert be a real stone if no one ever saw it?" is a silly question. We can assume that if no one ever saw the stone, the stone would still be there. Or, we can assume that the stone would *not* be there. But that has nothing to do with reality. The stone cannot be either *real* or *unreal*, except as it is perceived by someone. Reality is not a function of stones; it is a function of thought. Stones exist all over the world without ever being perceived by people. They are not concerned with whether they are real or not. They just go on being stones. *We* are the only ones who are concerned with whether they are real—and what we mean by that is, not "*are* they there?" but "can we *agree* about whether they are there?"

Of course, the agreement is easier if we go and look right at the stones instead of guessing about them. But the process of agreement is not different. Looking at the stones does not make them real or unreal; it only makes them easier to agree about. Two men could look at the stones, and one could say, "What pretty sponges." Poof! There goes the reality. "Well," you say, "he was just wrong." Exactly. He was wrong—that is, one of them was. But which one?

The answer is, the "wrong" one is the one who gets the smaller number of people to agree with him when he gets home. If he cannot get anyone to agree with him, he is very likely to be locked up in an institution for living in an unreal world. But the unreality of that world consists wholly and entirely of his lack of agreement with other people.

Let's assume that rocks are hard and water flows and all cats appear to be gray at night. It is easy for us to agree on this, but how can we demonstrate it in terms other than our own perceptions? We cannot. That is the hard fact. That is why reality is agreement.

The quickest way to drive someone insane is to do something to his reality, to introduce disagreements into his mind. Perhaps, if our civilization were built upon affinity or communication, this might not be the quickest way. But our civilization is built solidly upon agreements about the physical universe.[1] A man who looks at energy, space and time, and particularly matter, the way other men look at them, is sane. A man who looks at them differently is nuts. People are glad to tell him so. Therefore, we can cut off communication with people and make them angry. We can reverse affinity against them (i.e., express antipathy, dislike or rejection) and make them covertly hostile or grief-stricken. But when we produce disagreements in their minds about matter, energy, space and time, we drive them crazy.

---

[1] **physical universe:** a **universe** is the sphere or realm in which something exists or takes place. The **physical universe** is the universe of the planets, their rocks, rivers and oceans, etc. It is composed of Matter, Energy, Space and Time.

Imagine your own feelings if you were to walk into your office in the morning and find that your desk was removed, only to have your secretary, your boss, a receptionist and even the president of the company inform you quite bluntly that the desk was actually there. This is a denial of reality in a way that should not seem to affect you personally, but only two possible conclusions would be open to you: either you are crazy or they are crazy. There would be alternatives in between, such as, "They are playing a trick on me," but this would probably be called paranoia and the result would be the same. One of the first reactions you might have to a situation of this type would be that you were quite angry at the people who kept insisting your desk was there. If they continued to insist it was there and you decided it was hopeless to convince them otherwise, you might become quite apathetic. You would undoubtedly break off communication with these people.

COMMUNICATION

Communication, the last component of Understanding, is the heart of life. It is the interchange of ideas between two people or things. Without it we are dead to all.

A man's impact on the world has been directly proportionate to his development of a means of communication. Communication in its broadest sense, of course, includes all the ways in which a person or thing becomes aware of, or becomes aware to, another person or thing. Man's unusual ability to communicate in a number of different ways is largely responsible for the growth of his intelligence and the growth of his civilization. Before the development of language, man communicated quite readily and successfully by means of signs, gestures and imitation. Music is a very fine means of communication which can bypass the use of words completely. At the moment, however, language remains our most useful tool of communication. It is notable that the great men of history have almost unanimously been particularly adept at communication. A very large percentage of these men have used language as their primary means of communication.

There are two kinds of communication, both depending upon the viewpoint assumed. There is *outflowing* communication and *inflowing* communication. A person who is talking to somebody else is communicating *to* that person (we trust), and the person who is being talked to is receiving communication *from* that person. Now, as the conversation changes, we find the person who has been talked to is now doing the talking, and is talking *to* the first person, who is now receiving communication *from* him.

A conversation is the process of alternating outflowing and inflowing communication. There is a basic rule here: He who would outflow must inflow—he who would inflow must outflow. When we find this rule overbalanced in either direction we discover difficulty. A person who is only outflowing communication is actually not communicating at all in the fullest sense of the word. For in order to communicate entirely, he would have to inflow as well as outflow. Anyone who is talking, if he is not in a compulsive or obsessive state of beingness,[2] is dismayed when he does not get answers. Similarly, anyone who is being talked to is dismayed when he is not given an opportunity to give his replies.

---

[2] **beingness:** the condition of being; the result of having assumed an identity. It could be said to be "the role in a game." In the playing of a game, each player has his own **beingness**. One's own name, one's profession, one's physical characteristics — each or all of these things could be called one's **beingness**. [Example: *Jerry was so obsessed with his **beingness** as "The CEO", that he was oblivious to the fact that not one of his staff agreed with or even responded to his communication about his mission statement.*]

THE COMMUNICATION FORMULA

As we look at two people in communication, we can label one of them **A** and the other one of them **B**. In a good state of communication, **A** would outflow and **B** would receive. Then **B** would outflow and **A** would receive. Then **A** would outflow and **B** would receive. Then **B** would outflow and **A** would receive. In each case, both **A** and **B** would know that the communication was being received and would know what and where was the source of the communication.

All right, we have **A** and **B** facing each other in a communication. **A** outflows. His message goes across a distance to **B**, who inflows. In this phase of the communication, **A** is Cause, **B** is Effect, and the intervening space we term the Distance. Replied to, **A** is now the Effect and **B** is the Cause. Thus we have a cycle which completes a true communication. The cycle is:

Cause, *Distance*, *Effect* with *Effect* then becoming *Cause* and communicating across a *Distance* to the original *Cause* which is now *Effect*. And this we call a TWO-WAY COMMUNICATION.

As we examine this further, we find out that there are other factors involved. There is **A**'s *Intention*. This, at **B**, becomes *Attention*. And for a true communication to take place, a *Duplication* at **B** must take place of what emanated from **A**. **A**, of course, to emanate a communication, must have given Attention originally to **B**. And **B** must have given to this communication some Intention, at least to listen or receive. So we have both Cause and Effect having Intention and Attention.

The Communication Formula, then, is: *Cause*, *Distance*, *Effect*, with *Intention* and *Attention*, and a *Duplication* at *Effect* of what emanates from *Cause*. (Note: A communication, by definition, does not need to be two-way. When a communication is returned, the Formula is repeated, with Effect now becoming Cause and the former Cause now becoming Effect.)

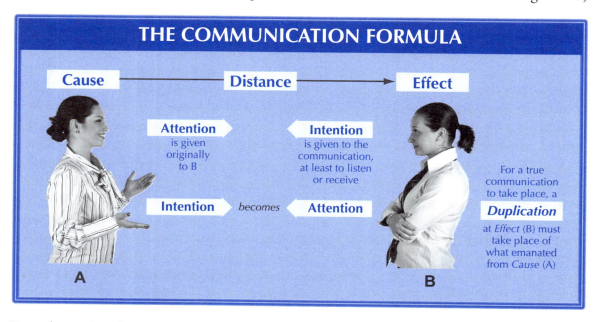

But what is Duplication? We could express this as "reality" or we could express this as "agreement". The degree of agreement reached between **A** and **B**, in this communication cycle, becomes their reality. And this is accomplished, mechanically, by Duplication. That is, as stated previously, reality is a function of thought.

Example: Sandy is having a conversation with Tim. She is telling him all about her recent Caribbean vacation. She describes an afternoon at the beach: *"The water was warm and inviting. It was so clear I could see the ocean floor. The sky was a deep blue, with a single, puffy white cloud lazily floating above, providing only brief shade from the relentless sunshine. A light sea breeze wafted over me as I lay on the white-sand beach."* Sandy's description was so vivid that Tim could almost smell the sea air. And that, in essence, is Duplication. Sandy's communication was such that Tim could "think" with it (duplicate it) and arrive at a shared "reality" with Sandy. The degree of reality reached in this communication cycle depends upon the degree of Duplication. For instance, if Sandy were to only describe the Caribbean beach in terms of how it compares to the shores of the Mediterranean, and if Tim has never been to the Mediterranean, the degree to which he duplicates her communication would be minimal and, consequently, the degree of reality would be very low. Furthermore, he could not then appropriately respond to Sandy's communication.

In two-way communication, **B**, as Effect, must to some degree Duplicate what emanated from **A**, as Cause, in order for the first part of the cycle to take effect. And then **A**, now as Effect, must Duplicate what emanated from **B** for the communication to be concluded. If this is done, there is no aberrative[3] consequence.

Where an unwillingness to send or receive communications occurs, where people obsessively or compulsively send communications without direction and without trying to be Duplicatable, where individuals in receipt of communications stand silent and do not acknowledge or reply, we have aberrative factors.

It might be seen by someone that the solution to communication is *not to communicate*. One might say that if he hadn't communicated in the first place, he wouldn't be in trouble now. "To communicate or not to communicate?" That is the question. If one got himself in such thorough trouble by communication, then of course one should stop communicating. But this is <u>not</u> the case. If one gets himself into trouble by communicating, he should further communicate. More communication, not less, is the answer.

Example: Curtis, an associate at an upscale specialty retail store, has been the top salesperson for the past two years. Last month, he sold a $3,500 espresso machine to a customer, for which he received a much-deserved commendation from Cindy, the store manager. She applauded his "can do" attitude and consummate professionalism. During a training meeting that same week, Cindy asked Curtis how he convinced the customer to purchase one of the most expensive items in the store. He told her that honoring an expired 20%-off coupon helped to close the sale. Upon hearing that, Cindy became quite upset because he violated corporate policy regarding expired coupons. She reprimanded Curtis severely in front of his coworkers and told him she would report his action to the regional manager and determine if disciplinary action should be taken. Curtis was both embarrassed and stunned by Cindy's treatment of him. He felt that he never should have mentioned the fact that the coupon had expired. He decided that the best thing for him to do is not to communicate at all with Cindy about his future sales...or anything else. The work environment became very stressful. Curtis' attitude worsened and, consequently, his sales declined. He was about to quit. Yesterday, feeling he had nothing to lose, he initiated a long overdue talk with Cindy that cleared the air. She apologized for overreacting and reprimanding him in front of others. Curtis

---

[3] **aberrative:** (*adj.*) marked by deviation from the proper or expected course of action. [Example: *Dave's doctor warned him that exceeding the recommended dosage of the medicine would lead to* **aberrative** *consequences, such as headaches and nausea.*]

promised to get permission before accepting expired coupons in the future. Following their talk, everything rapidly returned to normal. Curtis realized that he could have saved himself a lot of grief by communicating MORE, not less, at the time he got into trouble.

THE A-R-C TRIANGLE

These three words, *affinity*, *reality* and *communication*, do not seem on the surface to have much to do with each other. A little thought will discover that your affinity with another person will have something to do with your ability to communicate with him, but how these two are related to reality is not so easily seen. As a matter of fact, these three words have an extremely close and interesting relationship.

There is a triangle of considerable importance; an ability to use it gives a much greater understanding of life. The A-R-C Triangle is the common denominator to all of life's activities. The three corners of the triangle, represented by A, R and C, stand for Affinity, Reality and Communication, respectively.

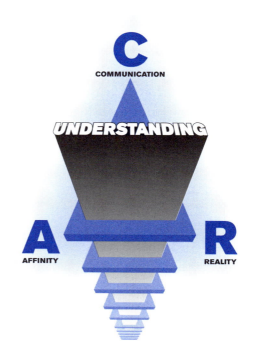

The interrelationship of the components of the triangle becomes apparent at once when one asks, "Have you ever tried to talk to an angry man?" Without a high degree of liking (*affinity*) and without some basis of agreement (*reality*), there is no *communication*. Without communication and some basis of emotional response, there can be no *reality*. Without some basis for agreement and communication, there can be no *affinity*. Thus we call these three things a *triangle*. Unless we have two corners of a triangle, there cannot be a third corner. Desiring any corner of the triangle, one must include the other two.

The triangle is not an equilateral (all sides the same) triangle. Affinity and reality are very much less important than communication. It might be said that the triangle begins with communication, which brings into existence affinity and reality.

Since each of these three aspects of existence is dependent on the other two, anything which affects one of these points will also similarly affect the others. It is very difficult to suffer a reversal of affinity without also suffering a blockage of communication and a consequent deterioration of reality.

ARC BREAKS

An *ARC break* (it is pronounced by its letters A-R-C break) is a sudden drop or cutting of one's affinity, reality or communication with someone or something. Upsets with people or things come about because of lessening or sundering[4] of affinity, reality, communication or understanding. It's called an *ARC break* instead of an *upset* because, if one discovers which of the three points of Understanding have been cut, one can bring about a rapid recovery in the person's state of mind.

Consider a lovers' quarrel: The husband comes home from work; he wants to see his wife and talk to her. While opening the door he anxiously yells out, "Hi, honey, I'm home!" He has offered affinity. The affinity is not acknowledged. She doesn't respond—just keeps on with her work in the kitchen. The husband can see her and feels she must have heard him. He feels insulted and begins to break off communication. He sits down and watches TV. Later on, the wife realizes her husband has been home for an hour and hasn't even talked to her yet! Not understanding this break-off, she also feels insulted and makes the break in communication even wider. They stop talking to each other and so they don't get the facts about what happened.

The area of agreement between the two inevitably diminishes and the reality of their relationship begins to go down. Since they no longer agree on reality, there is less possibility of affinity between them and the dwindling spiral[5] goes on.

This downward spiral can be started not only at the point of Affinity, but at any other point on the triangle. Regardless of which point lowers first, the other two points *always* lower as well.

RESTORING ARC

Fortunately, the spiral works both ways. When you raise one corner of the triangle, that will automatically raise the other two points. Anything which will raise the level of Affinity will also increase the ability to Communicate and add to the perception of Reality.

In the example above, let's say the husband is now sufficiently angry about his wife's apparent indifference to his arriving home and he confronts her about it. He asks her why she didn't respond to his greeting, to which she replies that she didn't hear him come in. She adds that the only reason she stopped talking to him was that she felt hurt that he had been home for an hour and didn't say a word to her. Realizing that it was all just a big misunderstanding, they apologize and embrace. They commence chatting away like nothing ever happened.

---

[4] **sundering:** breaking or wrenching apart; severing.

[5] **dwindling spiral:** The worse an individual or situation gets, the more capacity he or it has to get worse. ***Spiral*** refers to a progressive downward movement, marking a relentlessly deteriorating state of affairs, and considered to take the form of a **spiral.** The term comes from aviation, where it is used to describe the phenomenon of a plane descending and spiraling in smaller and smaller circles, as in an accident or feat of expert flying, which, if not handled, can result in loss of control and a crash.

With the communication re-established, affinity and reality were restored instantly!

Falling in love is a good example of the raising of the ability to communicate and of a heightened sense of reality occasioned by a sudden increase in affinity. If it has happened to you, you will remember the wonderful smell of the air, the feeling of affection for the good solid ground, the way in which the stars seemed to shine brighter and the sudden new ability in expressing yourself.

If you have ever been alone, and in a dwindling spiral, only to have the telephone ring and the voice of a friend come across, you will have experienced the halting of a downward spiral through a lift in communication. This is particularly true if the friend happens to be a person with whom you converse easily and who seems to understand the communication which you try to give him. After such an experience, you are probably aware of a great deal more interest in the things around you (reality) and the increase of the feelings of affinity within you.

Here's another example: A troopship filled with troops who had been overseas for several months was slowly approaching the Golden Gate Bridge. As the ship slowly approached the bridge, all on board grew very quiet until at last no one was talking at all. Suddenly, as though by prearranged signal, just as the bow of the ship cleared the bridge, the men in the front of the ship broke into a tremendous cheer which carried on down the length of the ship as she went under the bridge. Suddenly everyone was talking to one another excitedly. Men who scarcely knew each other were pounding each other on the back as though they were brothers. America regained some of its *reality* for these men and *communication* and *affinity* suddenly went up. Fast!

Unfortunately, the spontaneous incidents which cause affinity, reality and communication to increase are not as common as the incidents which *break* affinity, reality and communication.

Chapter 2
THE K-R-C TRIANGLE

In order to discover one's power and command of life, he must first understand the concepts of Knowledge, Responsibility and Control.

KNOWLEDGE

Knowledge is the fact or condition of being aware of something or knowing something with familiarity gained through experience or association. It can also be acquaintance with or understanding of a science, art or technique. The term *knowledge* applies to facts or ideas acquired by study, instruction, investigation, observation, experience or practical application.

RESPONSIBILITY

Responsibility is the ability and willingness to be Cause (i.e., the source-point). To accept responsibility for something is to accept that one operated as Cause in the matter. *Responsibility* should be clearly distinguished from such lower-level considerations as *blame* or *praise*, which include the further evaluation of the goodness or badness of the thing caused.

CONTROL

What is Control? Whether one handles a machine the size of a car or as small as a typewriter or even an accounting pen, one is faced with the problems of control. An object is of no use to anyone if it cannot be controlled. Just as a dancer must be able to control his body, so must a worker in an office or a factory be able to control *his* body, the machines of his work and, to some degree, the environment around him.

A person who is hatted[1] can control his job position. If he can control his job position, he can hold his position in space—in short, his location. If he can control his job position and its actions, he feels confident. He can work effectively and rapidly.

Take, for example, a court stenographer. The average length of time it takes for a stenographer to become proficient at recording courtroom testimony in real time is about three years. Have you ever seen or heard of a court reporter stopping the proceedings to tell the attorney to slow down or ask him to repeat what he said? No. A court reporter works effectively and rapidly. She controls her job and feels confident in doing so.

When a person is uncertain, he cannot control his job position, he cannot control his location. He feels weak. He goes slowly.

Consider a temp agency employee. Most often she would be someone who has some basic administrative skills, but would have to learn the specific functions of the temporary position while on the job. Let's say she's been hired to do some filing. Not really understanding the

---

[1] **hatted:** fully trained to do the specific functions of one's job.

company's filing system or the types of documents that need to be filed, she goes slowly. She asks a lot of questions. She makes a lot of mistakes and, consequently, she feels weak. The uncertainty results in her not really being able to control her job position. Furthermore, she cannot hold her position in space; e.g., she gets moved from place to place in the office and takes direction from people who aren't in charge to do things that aren't even part of her job. While the person supervising her would tolerate such poor performance because she is a "temp", that same supervisor would never tolerate that by a permanent employee doing the same job.

The key is CONTROL. Almost the entire subject of control is summed up in the ability to *start*, *change* and *stop* one's activities, body and his environment.

When one is hatted he knows the technology of HANDLING things. Thus he can control them. He is at CAUSE over his area.

THE K-R-C TRIANGLE

The points of the K-R-C Triangle are K for KNOWLEDGE, R for RESPONSIBILITY and C for CONTROL.

The K-R-C Triangle functions like the A-R-C Triangle. That is, when one corner is increased, the other two also rise. Furthermore, the K-R-C Triangle interacts best when used with high A-R-C.

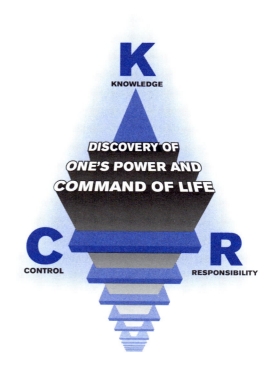

It is difficult to be responsible for something or control something unless you have KNOWLEDGE of it.

It is folly to try to control something or even know something without RESPONSIBILITY.

It is hard to fully know something or be responsible for something over which you have no CONTROL; otherwise the result can be an overwhelm.[2]

The route up from apathy or inaction is to *know* something about it, take some *responsibility* for the state one is in and the scene, and *control* oneself to a point where some control is put into the scene to make it go right. Then *know* why it went wrong, take *responsibility* for it and *control* it enough to make it go more toward an ideal scene.

---

[2] **overwhelm:** (*noun*) a state wherein one is overcome or overpowered in mind or feeling, so great as to make opposition (to a force, idea, concept, etc.) useless. [Example: *Dorothy realizes she has absolutely no control over the weather, and that she can't predict or prevent tornadoes, no matter how much she learns about them or how much responsibility she tries to take. Consequently, during tornado season, she ends up in an **overwhelm**.*]

Little by little, one can make anything go right by:

INCREASING KNOWLEDGE on all dynamics,[3]

INCREASING RESPONSIBILITY on all dynamics,

INCREASING CONTROL on all dynamics.

If one sorts out any situation one finds oneself in on this basis, he will generally succeed.

Most people have a dreadfully bad opinion of their capabilities compared to what they actually are. Hardly any person believes himself capable of what he is really capable of accomplishing.

When you play the game of life, you win some and you lose some. It's *how you handle the wins and losses* that makes all the difference.

By inching up each corner of the K-R-C Triangle bit by bit, ignoring the losses (don't dwell on failures along the way; no regrets) and making the wins firm (consolidate and strengthen your gains), a person eventually discovers his power and command of life.

Example: Darrell is an inventor who has wanted more than anything to invent something that will be of use to people and, in the process, allow him to make a good living from it. Over the past twenty years, he has developed and patented twelve unique products, ranging from a car seat for dogs to an automatic page-turner. While he exhibited great ingenuity, his ideas were never commercially successful. Despite his setbacks, he never dwelled on them. He ignored the losses and focused on what he learned from his experiences. Darrell was undaunted. Over the years, he increased his knowledge of mechanics, electronics and physics by taking night classes at the local college. He took the responsibility to find out what types of things people really *need* and *want* for improving their lifestyles, so that he wouldn't waste his time developing useless products. He focused his creative efforts in the areas he discovered from his research. Five years ago, Darrell decided to take more control of his career path by working part-time at his regular job and taking on an apprenticeship at a research and development company. During the past few years, Darrell became well known as a true innovator. His advice was heavily sought after. Whenever he experienced even the most minor successes, he ensured that he made his wins firm by getting news articles widely published about his efforts. Consequently, he became known as the "go-to guy" for cutting-edge concepts. In time, Darrell discovered his natural ability to inspire others and make their concepts a tangible reality. Last year, he started his own Internet-based consulting firm to help aspiring inventors transform their basic ideas into actual inventions. Through years of consistent application of the K-R-C Triangle, Darrell discovered his power and command of life; and in the process, he achieved all his life goals, both personal and financial.

It's quite easy to set a goal. But it takes courage to achieve it.

Courage could be summed up in: (1) being willing to cause something and (2) going ahead to achieve the effect one has decided to cause, against any and all odds. There just doesn't happen to be any such thing as failure. There isn't any reason to fail. There's no excuse for any failure that ever occurred, except this: There was just not quite enough carry-through and push-through.

---

[3] **dynamics:** There could be said to be eight urges (drives, impulses) in life. These are called **dynamics**. [See the definition of **dynamics** in the glossary on page 170 for a detailed explanation.]

Basic Organization

Chapter 3

UNDERSTANDING THE BASIC WORDS OF ORGANIZATION

Understanding ceases on going past a misunderstood word or concept.

If a person reading a text comes to a word or phrase he doesn't know, the words which appear thereafter may become "meaningless", "uninteresting" and he may even become slightly unconscious, his awareness shutting down.

Example: The president of a corporation is going to give a speech at the stockholders meeting at 9 a.m. tomorrow. He sent a note to Bill, his assistant, that states, *"Get a copy of the speech that Joe wrote for me, proofread it and delete any pejoratives you find, add the attached updates and have the corrected copy in my hands by 8 a.m."* Bill did not know the meaning of *pejoratives*, yet he didn't bother to find out that they are "words or phrases that have negative connotations, especially those that tend to belittle." Consequently, he failed to identify and delete any pejoratives contained in the speech. Furthermore, due to the misunderstood word he encountered, it didn't register that he was supposed to attach the updates. Bill felt groggy, so much so that he didn't even remember to get the speech to his boss by 8 o'clock the next morning.

In other words, when Bill encountered a misunderstood word, he ceased to understand and did not fully grasp or become aware of what followed thereafter.

All this applies to a sentence, a book, a job position or a whole organization.

ALL THIS IS THE MOST COMMON CAUSE OF UNACCEPTABLE PRODUCTION ON THE JOB, OR NO PRODUCTION AT ALL.

The difficulties of an organization in functioning or producing stem from this fact. The basic words of organization are glibly used but not generally comprehended—words like *company*, *management*, *technology*, *duties*, *hat*, *position* and *policy*.

Example: Marylou is a sales associate in a jewelry store. The owner of the store provided her with a policy manual when she started to work there two months ago. The manual clearly states that it is company policy for the sales associate to greet new customers as they enter the store. The manual also states that if the associate is busy with another customer, she is to tell the new customer she'll be with him momentarily. The policy further directs the sales associate to call for the floor manager in the event that she is unable to assist the new customer within five minutes. Unfortunately, Marylou did not fully comprehend the meaning of "policy". Instead of adhering to the policy as "a rule by which the company conducts its affairs", Marylou viewed *policy* to be merely a guideline or a goal to which the company aspires. Consequently, while busy attending to one customer, she would often ignore new customers who entered the store and she would fail to inform the manager that she couldn't help them. This resulted in many customers who walked in, browsed the merchandise and then left without buying anything. Sales were down 30% during the two months since Marylou was hired and no one realized that her misunderstanding of the meaning of "policy" led directly to the sharp decline in overall sales.

Vocabularies have to be increased before comprehension and communication occur and misunderstoods drop out.

Chapter 4
THE THEORY OF ORGANIZATION

The basic principles you have to know to organize[1] anything are contained in this chapter.

The whole theory of successful organization is to have job positions that only do specific things; to have sections,[2] departments[3] and divisions[4] which specialize; and to have people who only wear their own hats[5] and to know who is wearing the other hats in the company so he can send *their* work to them.

Organization consists of certain people doing certain jobs.

Disorganization consists of each person wearing all hats regardless of assignment.

But what is organization?

Most people have so many associated ideas with the word "organization" that they think of an organization as an identity or a being, not as a dynamic activity.

Let's see what an organization really is.

Take, for example, a pile of red, white and blue beads. Let's organize them. Now let's draw the organizing board,[6] indicating a person in charge of the activity.

Dump all the beads on top of "In-Charge", all mixed up in a confusion. Obviously In-Charge must *route* them to dig himself out. So we get:

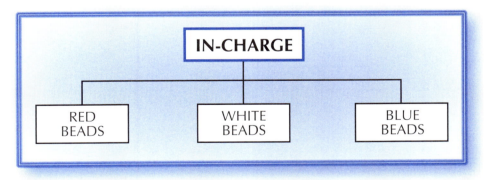

---

[1] **organize: 1.** to arrange in an orderly or systematic way. **2.** to set up an administrative structure for.

[2] **section:** a portion of a department.

[3] **department:** a portion of a division in an organization, headed by an executive, which is responsible for the performance of certain functions or production of certain products. [Examples: the Purchasing **Department**, the Printing **Department**]

[4] **division:** a part of an organization. [Examples: the research **division** of a company; the engineering **division** of a university]

[5] **hat:** slang for the title and work of a job position in an organization. Taken from the fact that in many professions such as railroading, the type of hat worn is the badge of the job. [Example: Mary wears two **hats** in her company, that of receptionist and mailroom clerk.]

[6] **organizing board:** a board which displays the functions, duties, sequences of action and authorities of an organization. The **organizing board** shows the pattern of organizing to obtain a product. The result of the whole **organizing board** is a product. The product of each hat on the board adds up to the total product of the organization. *Abbr.* **org board**.

Thus we find out much of what an in-charge does. He routes. He separates into types or classes of thing or action.

This, so far, is a motionless organization.

We have to have products.[7] Let's say its products are drilled beads, strung beads and polished beads.

We would get:

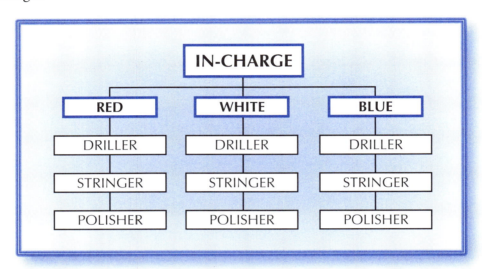

Or we would get:

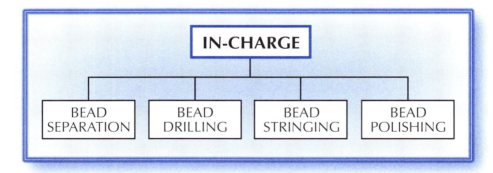

It is not particularly important which pattern of org board we use so long as it handles the volume of beads.

In a smooth organization that runs well and succeeds, EACH PERSON WEARS HIS OWN ASSIGNED HAT.

When a person has a job that belongs to another hat than his own, he passes the job to the other hat.

---

[7] **product:** a finished, high-quality service or article in the hands of the consumer as an exchange for a valuable.

Each member of an organization is a specialist. He specializes in his own hat.

Example: A train crew has a conductor; he wears a conductor's hat. It has an engineer; he wears the engineer's hat. It has a fireman;[8] he wears the fireman's hat. Where do you think the train would get to if each of these three didn't know who were the other two? The conductor wearing the engineer's hat would mean no fares. The fireman wearing the conductor's hat would mean no steam. And the engineer wearing the conductor's hat would mean no train going anywhere.

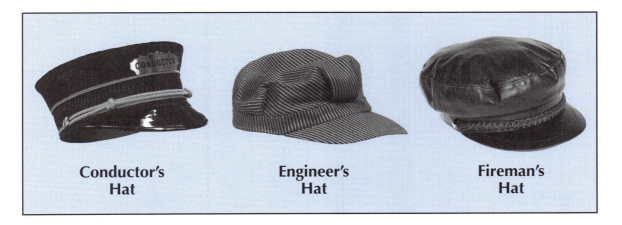

Conductor's Hat   **Engineer's Hat**   **Fireman's Hat**

If we only have one person in this "organization", he would still have to have some idea of organization and a sort of organizing board.

If we have any volume to handle we have to add people. If we add them without an org board we will also add confusion. The organization without an org board will break down by overload and cross-flows[9] and crosscurrents.[10] These in conflict become confusion.

So beware of wearing other hats than your own or being ignorant of what other hats are being worn. For nobody will go anywhere and you'll find yourself overworked, dismayed and unhappy.

Example: A flash flood hit the town of Riverside, engulfing 42 homes, causing widespread power outages and displacing more than 300 people. Riverside's emergency response team, consisting of eight city employees who hold those positions as additional duties in the event of natural disasters, immediately went into action. However, there was no organizing board detailing the specific responsibilities and functions of each team member in the event of an emergency. To add to the confusion, three of the eight emergency team members could not be located. Of those who responded, no one knew exactly what he was supposed to do. Consequently, one person took it upon himself to advise the National Guard to transport all evacuees to the sports stadium. Unfortunately, another team member directed all the relief supplies to be delivered to the convention center on the other side of town, so the evacuees were without food, water, cots and blankets. One person directed that injured

---

[8] **fireman:** the person who tends the fire of a steam engine; a stoker.

[9] **cross-flows:** actions that flow in a contrary direction.

[10] **crosscurrents:** actions counter to the main group activity.

people be taken to the county hospital, but another team member had already ordered that same hospital to be evacuated due to storm damage. Rather than sending the injured to several clinics throughout the town, that team member redirected all of them to a small outpatient clinic that immediately became overloaded and unable to treat the patients. The emergency team received several reports that evacuated homes had been looted. Each team member thought it was another's job to report that fact to the mayor, so no one did. Not informed of the actual situation, the mayor directed the police chief to beef up security at the local mall instead. This left dozens of homes without adequate police protection. In the final analysis, the lack of an organizing board for the emergency response team resulted in needless suffering, rampant crime and slow recovery.

All a confusion is, is unpatterned flow. The particles[11] collide, bounce off each other and stay IN the area. Thus there is no product, as to have a *product* something must flow OUT.

We can now note two things:

1. We have some stable items — these are ***job positions*** or ***locations***.

2. We have ***flow items*** — these are things undergoing ***change***.

So an organization's ***positions change flowing particles***.

Particles flow *in sequence*. Things enter an organization, get changed and flow out of an organization.

Any activity has a *sequence* of actions. It has to have stable points which do *not* flow in order to handle things which *do* flow.

It is not necessary to have a stable terminal[12] do only one thing. But if so, then it also has a correct sequence of actions.

All this is true of an engine room or a lawyer's office or any organization.

In an engine room, fuel flows in and is changed to motion which flows out. Somebody runs the machines. Somebody repairs the machines. It may all be done by one person, but as soon as volume goes up, one has to plan out the actions, classify them and put them on an org board which the people there know and abide by, or the place will not operate well.

---

[11] **particle:** a generic term used to describe any item being processed or handled in an organization, whether it be a person (e.g., a customer), a phone message, a memo, raw materials, etc.

[12] **terminal:** a point that receives, relays and sends communication or other particles in a company. A person located at such a point is commonly referred to as a **terminal**. A **stable terminal** is a person to whom programs, projects and orders may be given with the sure knowledge that they will be complied with and executed.

This is done by dividing operation and repair into two actions, making two activities on the same org board.

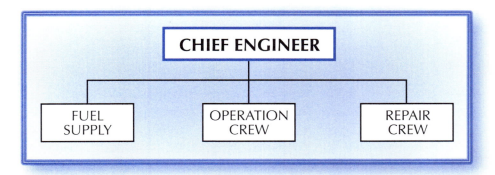

The Chief keeps the flows going and the terminals performing their actions.

In a lawyer's office we get different actions as a flow.

This would be a flow pattern, possibly with a different person (with a different skill) on each point.

So one *organizes* by:

1. Surveying (examining) the types of particles.

2. Working out the changes desired for each particle to make a product.

3. Posting[13] the terminals who will do the changing along the sequence of changes.

To be practical, an org board must also provide for pulling in the materials, disposing of the product and being paid for the cycle of action[14] and its supervision.

---

[13] **posting:** placing a person in an assigned area of responsibility and action, which is supervised in part by an executive.

[14] **cycle of action:** the *start-change-stop* of one's activities, body or his environment. [Example: *The sales division of a pottery manufacturing plant sold 500 flowerpots to a nursery. The plant manager, who is responsible for supervising the **cycle of action**, instructed (1) the purchaser to buy sufficient clay (**start**), (2) the craftsmen to make the flowerpots (**change**) and (3) the shipping department to deliver the items to the nursery (**stop**).*]

A company has various actions. It is essentially a collection of small org boards combined to operate together as a large org board.

To plan out *any* action, one has to be able to visualize its sequence of flows and the changes that occur at each point. One has to be able to see where a particle (paper, person, money) comes in and where it leaves. One has to be able to spot any point a particle will halt and be able to mend that part of the flow or handle it.

For that reason, it is just as vital to know an employee's whereabouts as it is to know what his duties and responsibilities are. For example, if someone plans to take a vacation, he should ensure that the receptionist knows when he'll be gone and to whom she should refer his calls during that period. He should also apprise coworkers within his department, who routinely interact with him during the course of business, that he will be out of the office. He must ensure that a specific individual or individuals will cover his job functions. This would also apply if he were taking sick leave or just taking the afternoon off to conduct personal business. Many companies use departmental sign-out boards as a way to keep track of employees' whereabouts. Just because one is absent, that doesn't mean that his job duties do not have to be performed. Most often, someone has to cover for a fellow employee who is absent from work. Failure to do so could lead to disruption of the proper flow of particles in an organization.

Case in point: Have you ever called a company, asking for your customer service rep by name, only to be placed on hold for five minutes while the receptionist tries to locate him? Then when she returns, she tells you that she can't find him or that he's out of the office. You then ask to speak to anyone else who could help you with your issue. The receptionist puts you on hold again, returning several minutes later, only to tell you that no one can help you other than the person for whom you called in the first place, that he is on vacation and that you will have to call back in a week when he returns. This is a clear example of a particle (you) that was halted (at reception) because no one in customer service had been named to cover for your rep in his absence. That part of the flow (from reception to customer service) must be mended or handled if that company expects to succeed.

A proper org board is a perpetual combination of flows which do not collide with one another and which do enter and do experience the desired change and which do leave as a product.

ORGANIZATIONAL GENIUS IS COMPOSED ONLY OF ARRANGING SEQUENCES OF ACTION AND DESIGNATING CHANNELS FOR TYPES OF PARTICLES. THAT'S ALL IT IS.

COPE[15] AND ORGANIZE

One, in actual practice, has to cope while organizing. It's perfectly all right to cope. One always must. But one MUST organize things while he copes.

If you *remain* in cope, the demand to cope increases. The mounting overload and overwhelm in an area comes entirely from cope-cope-cope without organizing also.

---

[15] **cope:** to handle any old way whatever comes up, to handle it successfully and somehow.

One begins to move out of cope by (1) putting an org board together that labels job positions and duties and (2) getting people in those positions to handle the types of particles of the organization. Any old org board is better than no org board at all. A good org board, well grooved in[16] with each employee and with duties well apportioned, permits things to smooth out and increase in volume without strain.

In a flood, if you can channel the water, you can handle the flood. If you just batter at water, you drown.

So cope by all means — but don't forget to organize a little each time you get a chance.

The end product of cope is drown. The end product of organize is freedom.

---

[16] **grooved in:** shown how something works so one can then operate it or handle it. Usually, a ***groove-in*** is a short action covering the basics of how something works or functions and is thus different from an apprenticeship, which is a longer, more detailed action.

Chapter 5

COMM LINES: DON'T JAM THEM

A communication line, or *comm line*, is the route along which a communication (particle, message, etc.) travels from one person to another. This does not refer to physical equipment (such as a telephone line or Internet cable) but to the passage of ideas between two points. It is the line on which flow memos,[1] voice originations and replies, information, requests, e-mails, etc.

To thoroughly understand the proper flow of communications in an organization, it is important for one to distinguish a *comm line* from a *command line*. This is best viewed in the context of an organizing board. [See illustration below.]

A comm line is horizontal, whereas a command line, a line on which authority flows (one on which orders[2] and directives travel from senior[3] to junior[4] and on which compliances travel from junior to senior), is vertical.

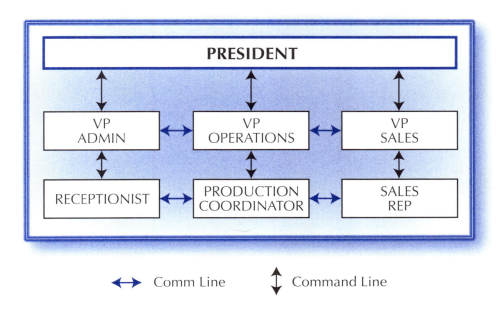

---

[1] **memo:** abbreviation for **memorandum**. A **memo** is a communication, usually brief, written for interoffice circulation. It may contain directive, advisory or informative matter.

[2] **order(s):** a direction or command issued by an authorized person to a person or group (section, department, etc.) within the sphere of the authorized person's authority. By implication, an **order** goes from a senior to juniors.

[3] **senior:** one's immediate superior in the workplace, i.e., the person to whom one reports directly in an organization; supervisor. [Example: *My **senior** gave me the day off.*]

[4] **junior:** an immediate subordinate employee; also referred to as a *direct report* in some companies. [Example: *John scheduled meetings with each of his **juniors** to evaluate their job performances.*]

Except when you've got to have speed, *never* use an interoffice phone to communicate with another member of your organization. Whenever possible, communication that *can* be put in writing *should* be put in writing. And never write a memo and present it *and you* at some other point at the same time. *Personally delivering* a memo is "off-line"[5] just as *using a phone* instead of sending a memo is "off-line".

A good use of the organization's communication lines reduces confusion. The other guy is busy, too. Why interrupt him or her unnecessarily with routine matters that should go on the memo lines?

A comm line can be *jammed*[6] in several ways:

1. **Entheta.**[7]

   The principal way a comm line can be jammed is by putting entheta on it. Ask yourself before it goes on the lines — *It's bad news, but is it necessarily important?*

   Example: Larry, the sales manager, and Tim, one of his sales reps, were having a heated argument in the company lunchroom. Mindy, an office assistant, walked into the room, just as the argument escalated into a shouting match, culminating with Tim swearing at his boss and storming out of the building. Larry instructed Mindy to refrain from telling anyone else what happened. Tim is the company's top salesman, responsible for 35% of the gross income, a fact Mindy knows very well. Despite the clear directive from Larry, Mindy felt that everyone should know that Tim blew up and possibly quit. She sent e-mails to many of her coworkers and spoke to others both on the phone and in person. The news spread like wildfire and by the end of the day, the only communication flowing on the lines was the now grossly exaggerated story of how Larry and Tim got into a fist fight and that Tim is going to sue the company. No work was getting done and all were worried that the company might start laying off people in anticipation of decreased sales.

2. **Overburden.**

   Too much traffic[8] jams a line. A memo that is too long doesn't get read.

---

[5] **off-line:** A **line** is a route along which a particle travels between one terminal and the next in an organization; it is a fixed pattern of terminals who originate and receive, or receive and relay, orders, information or other particles. A person is *on-line* when he uses the pattern of the organization correctly. If he does not, he is **off-line**. A particle, such as a memo, is **off-line** when it is sent to the wrong person. [See definition of **off-line** in the glossary on page 174 for examples.]

[6] **jam(med):** (*verb*) to block, congest or clog. [Example: *a drain that was **jammed** by debris*]

[7] **entheta:** [*en-*, enturbulated + **theta**, thought or life. *Enturbulated*: caused to be turbulent or agitated and disturbed. *Theta*, the eighth letter of the Greek alphabet, means *thought* or *life* or *the spirit*.] **Entheta** means irrational or confused or destructive thought. It especially refers to communications, which, based on lies and confusions, are slanderous, choppy or destructive. **Entheta** can also consist of anger, sarcasm, despair or slyly destructive suggestions.

[8] **traffic:** communication, dealings or contact between persons or groups.

Example: The owner of a consulting firm received a letter of complaint from one of the company's clients regarding lack of service. He investigated the matter and found that her consultant had indeed canceled three appointments in a row. Concerned that other clients might have experienced poor or no service, the owner directed all employees of his company to write reports to the Quality Control (QC) division detailing any information they might have regarding client dissatisfaction with any of the company's twelve consultants. Within 48 hours, Quality Control received 62 reports, most of which concerned issues that had already been resolved and even issues that had nothing to do with client dissatisfaction. There were multiple reports written about the same client. It took QC personnel several days to sort through all of them. Five of the reports were so long that they never even got read. In the process, many important documents that the division should have addressed immediately were mixed in with all the other traffic and did not get handled in a timely manner. The 62 reports that inundated Quality Control jammed the line to that division.

Note: Regarding e-mail in-boxes, it is not at all unusual to find important communication buried among dozens, if not hundreds, of unnecessary and unsolicited e-mails. One reason this occurs is that, when one sends an e-mail, it is quite easy to CC[9] multiple recipients, whether they have a need to know or not. Therefore, care should be taken to address your e-mails only to those individuals who, by their position and duties in the company, should receive your communication. Failure to do so could contribute to the overburdening of comm lines.

3. ***Too Little Data.***

That can jam a line but thoroughly. It takes more memos to find out what's going on.

Example: Laurie is the Finance Director for a large corporation. She is working on the annual budget and needs input from all the department heads regarding their proposed expenditures for the coming year. She sent each one a memo requesting precise figures for salary projections, as well as expenditures for office supplies, durable equipment, etc. Mark, the head of Information Systems, wrote, *"The new computer network has been ordered."* He provided no specifics. Laurie wrote back asking, *"What computer network? Who authorized the expenditure? How much does it cost?"* Mark simply replied, *"The one we discussed two months ago. I got it for 20% off the list price."* Laurie still had no idea what he was referring to. She exchanged a dozen memos with Mark before she found out what was going on! Furthermore, she spent the entire afternoon trying to extract the other data she needed from Mark to do her budget projections. She never got a chance to look at the memos from the 15 other department heads. The exchange of memos with Mark thoroughly jammed the line to Laurie.

---

[9] **CC:** [**C**arbon **C**opy] the field in an e-mail header that names additional recipients for the message.

4. ***Bypass The Line Itself.***

   When one fails to utilize a communication line that *should be* utilized (in accordance with the correct pattern of the organization or company policy), that comm line is said to have been *bypassed*. This typically occurs when the originator of a communication fails to route the particle to each of the appropriate recipients or when he sends it to the wrong terminal altogether. Consequently, the person who should be receiving data that is pertinent and vital to his job has been blocked from receiving it. Whereas *too much traffic* and *too little data* jam a line, being *bypassed* jams the terminal, i.e., he gets stuck or immobilized, unable to do his job properly or at all.

   Example: Jesse is the most in-demand personal trainer at a private health club. A standing company policy dictates that if a prospective club member specifies that he will only join the club on the condition that he would be able to retain Jesse's services, then he must be scheduled for an introductory appointment with Jesse prior to being signed up for membership. Management wrote the policy to ensure that Jesse would be able to meet the clients' specific needs and that he would be available to train them. Pam, the sales rep, is fully aware of the policy. However, her production level has been down lately and so she decided to bypass the appointment with Jesse when signing up six new customers this week, all of whom indicated a desire to work with him. When the new members arrived for the first time to the club, each requested to be placed in Jesse's appointment book three times a week. Jesse was taken completely by surprise. He did not have room in his book to accommodate six new clients. He tried to work something out with each client, to include rescheduling existing clients, so that everyone could be trained. However, it was not possible. Three of the new members quit on the spot and demanded a refund. Jesse was able to accommodate the others, but he had to completely reorganize his schedule to do so and reluctantly extend his work week by five hours. Pam's off-policy action of bypassing the comm line to Jesse made it impossible for him to do his job properly.

5. ***Erroneous Data.***

   Putting erroneous data on the comm line is a pet hate[10] of many people. Generally its form is *"everybody knows"*.

   Example: *"They say that George is doing a bad job,"* or *"Nobody liked the last newsletter."* The proper rejoinder is *"Who is Everybody?"* You'll find it was one person who had a name. When you relay negative or critical data, omit the *"everybody"* generality. Say who. Say where. Otherwise, you'll give somebody the wrong idea.

---

[10] **pet hate:** *(idiom) British English,* also **pet peeve** *American English,* something that is disliked intensely and is a constant or repeated annoyance.

Chapter 6
WHAT AN EXECUTIVE WANTS ON HIS LINES

The role of an executive is to plan and execute actions and to coordinate activities. To do this he gets people to do their jobs and establishes the overall plan of action. Only an executive can string lines[1] and coordinate actions and resolve the jams that impede things.

To jam an executive's communication lines is a serious thing to do. The result is a cut line. A bottleneck is created by employees when they jam a line to an executive. Eating up an executive's time and patience destroys harmony, promotion, marketing and income.

An executive does not want on his incoming communication lines:

1. **Demands for decisions**

    Demands for decision are always indicative of irresponsibility; people want the executive to make the mistakes; and an executive *can* make mistakes if he is asked to make decisions distant from his zone of action, equipped with insufficient data to make the decision correctly. For an executive to decide for people those decisions that are applicable only to the sphere of *one* job is folly. Depending on an executive for petty decisions is sure to jam lines and cost income.

2. **Backflashes and can'ts**

    A backflash, by definition, is an unnecessary response to an order. This can get fairly wicked. Backflashes are not acknowledgments; they are comments or refutals.

    Example: *"Sell the bricks"* as an order is replied to by *"Bricks are hard to sell"* or *"We should have sold them yesterday."* This is a disease peculiar to only a few employees. They cannot receive an order directly and are seeking to be part of the communication, not the recipient.

---

[1] **string a line:** (*idiom*) to establish a fixed pattern of terminals who originate and receive, or receive and relay, orders, information or other particles. [Example: *For his new brochure project, the marketing director **strung a line** between the account rep and the graphic design artist so that client input regarding content would be taken into account when designing the brochure.*]

This goes so far as senseless "Wilco's"[2] or "I'll take care of it" when the executive only wants to know "Is it done?"

Memos or orders, in most instances, are held by the recipient until completed. The executive who issues an order assumes that it got through.

The recipient doesn't need to return the order with a senseless "Will do" or "You can count on me!" written on it. Since the executive only wants to know that the order has been complied with, he would consider any response short of compliance to be backflash.

That said, it occasionally happens that an order is issued or a policy is enforced or is found to exist which, if put into full effect in a certain area, would result in loss or destruction.

Instead of putting the order into effect, the recipient should query (to put a question to someone in order to express one's doubts about something or to check its validity or accuracy) the order with

a. the name of the issuer and the exact order,

b. the reason it would result in loss or destruction if put into effect,

c. a recommendation resolving the problem the order sought to solve.

Noncompliance as a method of avoiding a destructive order is very risky. It is far, far better, in writing, to make the above submission.

Example: Eric, the marketing division manager at Ace Plumbing, observed that during the past quarter, there has been a steady increase in requests by customers for a free estimate, which the company has advertised since it opened its doors for business twelve years ago. While Eric was happy with the 42% increase in public reach for their services, that translated into only a 7% increase in new contracts. Historically, the company has experienced a conversion rate (from providing a free estimate to making the sale) of 68%. Recently, that percentage has dropped by nearly half to just 35%. The cost to the company, in terms of time and travel to do free estimates for so many people that did not result in sales, was of concern to management. So Eric decided to change the longstanding policy of doing free estimates. He issued an order to Valerie, the head of Advertising, to remove that offer from all ads. Valerie knows how successful the free estimate offer has been. She felt that discontinuing it was shortsighted and would be quite destructive to the company financially. So she queried the order. She stated that she doesn't agree with Eric's decision and that it could very well result in loss of business. She added that, from her experience, offering free estimates has set the company apart from the competition and, until recently, has been quite profitable. She recommended that the company instead focus on the person in the office who takes the calls and schedules the free estimates to see if there has been a change in how those calls are being handled. Valerie believed that an inspection into that area should be done before making such a drastic change in marketing. Eric reconsidered. He agreed with her recommendation. Upon investigation, it was found that about three months ago, the call taker had discontinued using the approved script for handling requests for free estimates. The call taker was immediately retrained and drilled on proper procedure. Not surprisingly, during the next month, the number of free estimates scheduled dropped a bit, but the conversion rate shot up to 75%, higher than it had been in years.

---

[2] **wilco:** (*interjection*) [**wil**l **co**mply] an expression used especially in radio communications to indicate agreement or compliance.

The query should go to the issuer in the format outlined above. If it is still insisted upon and still is destructive, send it and all particulars to the person who is authorized per your company policy to adjudicate the matter (e.g., the office manager, executive director, etc.). Label it DESTRUCTIVE ORDER and ask for help in handling. Refuse meanwhile to put it into effect. If the executive director or CEO issues an order you find to be destructive and upon query he still insists it be followed, report the matter to the senior-most authority of the organization (e.g., the owner or the board of directors).

Going ahead and putting the order into effect, even though it means loss and destruction, without advising anyone is itself very destructive. IT DOES NOT RELIEVE ONE OF RESPONSIBILITY WHEN ONE EXECUTES A DESTRUCTIVE ORDER. The one who follows it is in fact far more guilty than the issuer since the one following it is right there, able to OBSERVE, whereas the issuer may not be.

Using this policy to avoid routine actions plainly not resulting in loss or destruction, WHICH NOT DONE do result in loss or destruction, can result in an investigation and the one who refused the order can be held at fault for any resulting destruction. This policy mainly applies to new, nonroutine orders or attempted changes.

In the matter of *can'ts*, an executive seldom orders the impossible and generally consults with people before issuing an order. A persistent "Can't be done" means "I am unwilling."

3. **Entheta**

   Entheta means embroidered[3] reports. Data is data. It is not opinion. Data, not entheta, brings about action. All entheta does is cut the communication lines.

   Example: Sherry sells window blinds and shades at an upscale store. She was on the phone taking a very detailed and lengthy order from a client when her computer froze. She had to restart the computer, losing in the process all the data she had entered for the past twenty minutes. The client was understanding, but couldn't remain on the line any longer. She said she'd have to place the order at another time. When the call ended, Sherry burst into her supervisor's office and shouted, *"The computer crashed and I lost a very big sale!"* The supervisor, Victoria, asked Sherry what she was talking about. Sherry told her that she was writing up a big order when the computer crashed, and that the client became enraged and stated she would take her business elsewhere. Sherry told Victoria that the client said she would never patronize the store again. Sherry then proceeded to tell Victoria that she was fed up with how antiquated the computer system is and that this never should have happened. She added that she has experienced many other episodes of computer problems that caused her to lose business, and that she believed that the company has lost a tremendous amount of income due to computer malfunction. None of that was true, but Sherry surmised that she would have to embellish what happened in order to get Victoria's attention and to get her to take immediate action. Unfortunately, Sherry's behavior had the opposite effect. Victoria was so put off by her ranting, that all she did was order Sherry to get out of her office. Thereafter, Victoria forbade Sherry from speaking to her directly about anything. Sherry had to go through Victoria's assistant for any requests, no matter how urgent. Sherry wanted to get immediate action, but all she succeeded in doing was to upset Victoria with exaggerated reports, resulting in Victoria cutting the line between Sherry and her.

---

[3] **embroidered:** embellished with fictitious additions or exaggerations.

WHAT AN EXECUTIVE'S LINES SHOULD LOOK LIKE

There are only four things which an executive wants on his incoming communication lines.

These are:

1. **Information**

    When a member of an organization does something of importance, he should always inform the executive after the fact. It is perfectly all right to take actions within one's organizational purpose.[4] It is not all right to keep it a secret.

    a. Do it.

    b. Tell the right people and the executive by adequate communication at the speed necessary to the case.

    Similarly, an executive ought to tell people his goals and plans; and when he does something of any importance to others, he ought to say so. The captain who tells the ship's officers and crew how the action is going saves a lot of nerves and useless motion.

2. **Appointments and dismissals of personnel for his action or confirmation**

    Minor hirings and firings in a department by authorized persons should always be subject to confirmation by a senior executive at least after the fact. Major appointments and dismissals of key personnel must be okayed by a senior executive before the fact, and action taken only on the senior executive's authority.

3. **Financial matters**

    Executives have varying degrees of financial responsibility, depending on their role in the organization. Financial matters that are typically of concern to an executive include authorization for capital expenditures, changes to long-range financial planning and payment of bills. Generally, any matter affecting the financial health of the organization is an executive matter.

4. **Acknowledgments**

    An acknowledgment is something said or done to inform another that his statement or action has been noted, understood and received. An acknowledgment also tends to confirm that the statement has been made or the action has been done, and so brings about a condition not only of communication, but of reality between two or more people.

    As previously noted, acknowledgments are not the same as comments or refutals.

    Example: If an executive orders an employee to *"Sell the bricks"* and the employee replies, *"Bricks are hard to sell,"* that would be a comment (i.e., the employee is seeking to be part of the communication). If he replies, *"Yes, sir"* or *"Okay"*, that would be an acknowledgment (i.e., the employee is being only the recipient of the communication).

---

[4] **purpose:** the entire concept of an ideal scene for any activity. [Example: *Lisa's organizational **purpose** as the receptionist is to receive particles of all types and route them expeditiously to the appropriate terminals, according to the organizing board.*]

Chapter 7

YOUR JOB AND HOW TO KEEP IT

WHAT IS YOUR JOB?

Anything in an organization is your job if it lessens the confusion if you do it.

Your doing exactly the duties required by your job position and using your exact comm lines lessens confusion. *But* failure to wear another hat that isn't yours now and then may cause more confusion than doing *only* your job.

The question when you see you will have to handle something not yours is this: "Will it cause less confusion to handle it or to slam it back onto its proper lines?"

Answer it by deciding which is less confusing. You'll find out by experience that you can create confusion by handling another's particles, *but* you will also discover that you can create confusion by *not* handling another's particles on occasion.

Example: The hostess at a trendy restaurant seats a party of four for dinner. Jeremy, the server who is responsible for the table at which they're seated, is swamped with customers. He hasn't even noticed that they were placed at one of his tables. The hostess doesn't notice that although 15 minutes has passed since she seated the party, there are still no drinks on the table. Fortunately, Connie, another server on the floor, has observed the guests looking anxiously about the dining room. They appear to be irritated at the lack of service. She sees that the hostess is unaware of what's going on and that Jeremy has his hands full. Connie realizes that confusion and upset are about to ensue because those customers don't even know who their server is. She decides that it would be less confusing if she were to initially wait on them herself, taking their drink and appetizer orders, and also telling them that their waiter, Jeremy, will be with them shortly. She makes sure the orders are placed and then goes back to handling her own station. But before she does, she tells Jeremy exactly what his customers ordered, so that he doesn't cause further upset by asking them for their drink and appetizer orders again.

The only real error you can make in handling another's particles is to fail to tell him by verbal or written communication *exactly* what you did. You stole his hat for a moment. Well, always give it back.

Usually, an employee has to know more jobs in the company than his own, particularly jobs adjacent to his position on the org board. He often has to do more jobs than his own because those jobs simply have to be done, no one else is there to do them and he sees that. He is only limited in what he can do in the organization by lack of know-how.

Example: Mary is a well-trained, proficient billing and collections clerk in a dental practice. The duties of her own job do not extend beyond the handling of finances and she performs her job in the back office. Yesterday, the front desk person didn't show up for work. Mary took it upon herself to move her files to the front desk and she proceeded to greet patients and answer the phones for the rest of the day, while getting her own work done in the process. After lunch, the dental assistant became ill; she went home an hour early. There was still one patient left to treat and with no one else in the office besides the dentist, she performed the duties of his assistant for that one patient. She saved the day in more ways than one. Mary was not only experienced in her own job, but she had also learned how to help out in a pinch in both the front office and the treatment room.

So, an employee gets the job done of (1) his own position, (2) his department and (3) the whole organization. An employee must always make sure that he thoroughly does his own job before helping to get other jobs done in his department or elsewhere in the organization. While it is certainly okay to help out when needed in other areas of the company, there can be extremes here. People who are *always* off-line and drifting about into the areas of other people, wasting the time of others and getting in their hair, aren't doing their own jobs. When we find somebody doing that, we know if we look in *his* area we'll find a rat's nest.[1]

HOW TO KEEP YOUR JOB

Your hat is your hat. It is to be worn. Know it, understand it, do it. Make the title and duties of your job position known to others in your organization. Ensure they understand precisely what it is you do.

You keep your job in a good organization by *doing* your job. There should be no further politics involved. So, in a well-run company, if you do your job you've got a job. And that's the way it should be.

---

[1] **rat's nest:** (*informal*) a place of great clutter or disorder.

Chapter 8

ORGANIZATION AND MORALE

Morale, regarded as a characteristic of an organization, is a sense of common purpose or a degree of dedication to a common task. Morale may also be defined as a confident, resolute, willing, often self-sacrificing and courageous attitude of an individual toward the function or tasks demanded or expected of him by his group. That attitude is based upon such factors as pride in achievement, pride in the aims of the group, faith in its leadership and ultimate success, a sense of fruitful personal participation in its work and a devotion and loyalty to other members of the group.

Morale is a large factor in organizing. An executive is utterly dependent upon the willingness of those who work for him. Willingness, while it is a factor in morale, is also a manifestation of morale. That is, the mere fact that morale exists in a group is an indication that willingness is present.

Good morale is the product of good organization! Organizing is the know-how of changing things. If you organize something well and efficiently, you will have good morale. You will also have improved conditions. If you find a company or portion of a company exhibiting bad morale, the solution is to put better organization into that area. Wherever morale is bad, organize!

There's nothing at all wrong with righting evil conditions — far from it. But if you want to better things, KNOW HOW TO ORGANIZE.

A very careful survey of people shows that their basic protests are against lack of organization. "It doesn't run right!" is the reason they protest things. Inequalities of workload, rewards unearned, no havingness[1] — these are some of the things that are snarled about. They are cured by organizing things.

Wherever you see bad morale, behind it you will see chaotic disorganization. A nation or an organization follows the same laws. Bad organization equals bad morale. Good organization equals good morale. And good organization is something worked on by a group, not ordered

---

[1] **havingness:** the feeling that one owns or possesses. In an organization, one's **havingness** could be achieved or increased by such things as a pay raise, new health benefits, a bonus, earned rewards, recognition or stock in the company.

under threat of severe penalty. The only people who blow their tops[2] when effective organization starts going in (i.e., when personnel and materials are effectively arranged in an orderly or systematic way) are those who take delight in suppression and don't want others to have things. In other words, good organization is only opposed by those who have reason to fear others. For in organization lies the secret of a group's strength.

A small group thoroughly organized can conquer the disorganized billions — and have excellent morale while they're doing it!

---

[2] **blow (one's) top:** (*idiom*) **1.** fly into a rage; lose one's composure. **Top** refers to the top of an erupting volcano. [Example: *If she calls about this one more time, I'm going to **blow my top**.*] **2.** go crazy, become insane.

Products and Exchange

Chapter 9

PRODUCTS AND SUBPRODUCTS

PRODUCT DEFINED

A product is a finished, high-quality service or article in the hands of the consumer as an exchange for a valuable.

Example: Dan is a carpenter. He builds kitchen and bathroom cabinetry. Deborah hired Dan to replace her kitchen cabinetry with solid wood cabinets (*article*) for an agreed-upon amount of money (*a valuable*). He constructed beautiful cherry wood cabinets (*high quality*), finely sanded and sealed with three coats of varnish and decorated with elegant stainless steel hardware (*finished*). Dan's installation of the cabinetry (*in the hands of the consumer*) was flawless. Deborah loved his workmanship and she gladly paid him for his work (*exchange*).

Unless it's exchangeable it's not a *product* at all. Product is exchange, exchange is product.

Example: Gary is an artist; he paints with oils. His works have sold well at a gallery owned by Susan. Recently, Gary decided to paint a series of landscapes, which is quite a departure from the modern art for which he's well known. Susan displayed his landscapes in her gallery for a month and not one piece sold. She finally had to remove the pieces and return them to Gary to make room for artwork that would sell. Even though Gary's art pieces are finished, high-quality articles, they are not PRODUCTS because they are not "in the hands of the consumer as an exchange for a valuable".

Even the individual has to put his service or article in the hands of some other employee before it could be called a *product*.

Example: Lucy works in a chiropractic office. Her job is to keep the schedule book filled, verify insurance coverage prior to the appointments and ensure the patients arrive on time. Last week, Lucy filled the entire appointment book, verified all insurance data and got 95% of the patients to arrive for their appointments. The office manager was thrilled with her production. Lucy met the definition of *product*, in that her services were finished, high quality and in the hands of her coworkers. She provided an exchange for the valuable (her pay) that she received.

On the other hand, let's say that Lucy failed to obtain the required insurance information from any of the patients. She did not turn over to the billing clerk the vital data she required for prompt and correct billing. In that case, Lucy could not call that aspect of her job (verifying insurance coverage) a product, as she didn't put it in the hands of some other employee, namely the billing clerk.

NAME, WANT AND GET YOUR PRODUCT

Products don't ever happen by themselves. You have to name them (i.e., specify what your products are), want them and get them.

NAME

Breaking this down into its parts we find that the most common failure of any employee lies in the first item, NAME YOUR PRODUCT!

On org boards, one has products listed. Every employee has one or more products. When you see personnel whirling around and dashing into walls and each other and not producing a thing, chances are, few of them can NAME what products they are trying to produce.

IF PRODUCTION IS NOT OCCURRING, THE ABILITY TO NAME THE PRODUCT IS PROBABLY MISSING.

WANT

One has to actually WANT the product he is asking for or is trying to produce. One does not have to be in a passionate, mystic daze about wanting the product. But one shouldn't be moving mountains in the road of a guy trying to carry some lumber to the building site either.

GET

To GET, you have to know how to organize. One has to spend some time organizing in many different ways — the organization itself, the hatting, the technical skill employees would have to have — to get anywhere in GETTING a product. A manager looks pretty silly trying to order a brick wall built when he doesn't have any bricks or bricklayer and provides no means at all of obtaining either one.

Sure, if you only organize and never produce, you never get a product either. But if you only produce and never organize, the only brick wall you'll ever see is the one you run into.

VALUABLE FINAL PRODUCTS

By definition, a valuable final product is something that can be exchanged with other activities (e.g., a division, a company, a community, etc.) in return for support. The support usually adds up to food, clothing, shelter, money, tolerance and cooperation (goodwill).

On an individual basis this is easy to grasp. The individual produces a product or products which, flowed into the department, division, organization, company, community, state, nation or planet, then returns to him his pay and goodwill or at least sufficient goodwill to prevent his abandonment or destruction. Long-range survival of the individual is attained in this fashion.

A valuable final product (VFP) is *valuable* because it is potentially or factually exchangeable. The key word in this sense is EXCHANGEABLE. And exchangeability means *outside*, with something *outside* the person or activity (an organizational unit, e.g., section, department). A valuable final product could as easily be named a VALUABLE EXCHANGEABLE PRODUCT.

Parts of organizations, organizations, towns, states and countries all follow the principles which apply to the individual. The survival or value of any section, department, division or organization is whether or not it follows these principles of exchange. Therefore it is vital that a person or a section, department, division, part of an organization or an organization figures out exactly what it is exchanging. It is producing something that is valuable to the activity or activities with which it is in communication and for doing that it is obtaining support. If it is actually producing valuable final products, then it is entitled to support.

The basics of valuable final products are true for any industrial or political or economic system. Many systems attempt to avoid these basics, and in such cases, the end result would be disaster. The individual, section, department, division, organization or country that is not producing something valuable enough to exchange will not be supported for long. It is as simple as that.

COMPILING A SUBPRODUCT LIST

If a person or any part of his company is only organizing or hoping or PRing[1] and is not producing an exchangeable commodity or commodities in VOLUME or QUALITY for which support can be elicited and even demanded, that person or part of the company will not be VIABLE (capable of success or continuing effectiveness). It doesn't matter how many orders are issued or how well org boards are drawn or beautiful the plans to produce are made. The hard fact of production remains the dominant fact.

How well organized things are *increases* production volume and *improves* quality and thus can bring about viability.[2] But it is the valuable final product, there and being exchanged, that determines basic survival. Lack of viability can always be traced to the volume and quality of an actual valuable final product.

---

[1] **PRing: PR** [**P**ublic **R**elations] is *good works well publicized*. It consists of those functions of a corporation, organization, etc., concerned with attempting to create favorable public opinion for itself. **PR** can be corrupted to "a technique of lying convincingly." Used as a slang expression, **PRing** means putting up a lot of false reports to serve as a smoke screen for idleness or bad actions. [Example: *John was having quite a lot of trouble making his sales quota. He was merely* **PRing** *his boss when he said that he expected to have his best month ever.*]

[2] **viability:** the longevity, usefulness and desirability of the product. **Viability** depends, in the main, upon exchange where economics are concerned.

Hope of a product has a short-term value that permits an activity to be built. But when the hope does not materialize into a product, then any hoped-for viability also collapses. One then must organize *back* from the actually produced product.

If you take any VFP and trace it backwards step by step, using a BE–DO–HAVE breakdown of what it took to create it, and then wrote up the list as preliminaries (i.e., the sequential actions that result in the VFP), you would have a subproduct list.

Example: Mark is a seminar coordinator. He's in charge of setting up seminars for his company at hotel conference rooms throughout the country. The seminars must be scheduled three months in advance and result in maximum attendance with all required personnel and materials present. His VFP is "Well planned and successfully delivered seminars."

The minimum subproducts list would divide into what he had to BE, what he had to DO and what he had to HAVE to wind up with a well planned and successfully delivered seminar:

SEMINAR COORDINATOR'S SUBPRODUCT LIST

Be:
- Someone who wants to coordinate seminars
- Someone hatted to coordinate seminars
- Someone who is capable of improvising and adapting on the spot

Do:
- Select city and reserve hotel for seminar
- Get list of staff to attend
- Schedule flights
- Arrange ground transportation
- Get budget funded
- Confirm all attendees
- Mail welcome packets
- Ship seminar packs and brochures to hotel
- Arrive at hotel one day in advance
- Ensure all materials are present
- Set up conference room
- Test the audiovisual equipment
- Greet clients
- Assist seminar speakers as needed

Have:
- Money for seminar expenses
- Time to schedule seminar far in advance
- National hotel directory
- Telephone
- Client contact list
- Internet / e-mail access
- Flight schedules
- Packing materials
- Seminar packs & brochures
- Conference room
- Audiovisual equipment
- Cell phone

If, at some future date, Mark found out there was something wrong with his valuable final product, all he would have to do is assess this list and find out why no VFP. The subproducts that he omitted and the wrong objectives that he pursued would leap from the page at him and, if handled, could result in his VFP quite promptly.

A valid subproduct list will greatly increase organization efficiency and show up holes. As it is VFPs which keep an organization going, not promises or hope, you can see that a subproduct list is vital to straighten out an area.

By assessing the subproduct list against a direct inspection of the area to which it applies, one can see the major things that are missing. It is these missing things which are preventing the attainment of the valuable final product of the area, so vital to the organization's survival.

The test of any subproduct list is: Is it resulting in VFPs? If not, somebody has been busy making a staff busy (i.e., with busywork – work that consumes time but doesn't yield productive results). The test of a correct subproduct list is: Does it result in good VFPs when used?

Chapter 10

EXCHANGE, COMPANY INCOME AND PAYROLL

Sometimes the problem of "meeting payroll" arises. So it is of interest what really underlies company income and payroll. There is a term used in business called "fair exchange." Let us apply this to a company engaged in servicing the public.

We could isolate four conditions of exchange:

1. First consider a group that takes in money but does not deliver anything in exchange. This is called *rip-off*. It is the "exchange" condition of robbers and other criminal elements.

2. Second is the condition of *partial exchange*. The group takes in orders or money for goods and then delivers part of it or a corrupted version of what was ordered. This is called short-changing or "running into debt" in that more and more is owed, in service or goods, by the group.

3. The third condition is the exchange known, legally and in business practice, as ***fair exchange***. One takes in orders and money and delivers exactly what has been ordered. Most successful businesses and activities work on the basis of "fair exchange".

4. The fourth condition of exchange is not common but could be called ***exchange in abundance***. Here one does not give two for one or free service but gives something more valuable than money was received for.

   Example: The group has diamonds for sale; an average diamond is ordered; the group delivers a blue-white diamond above average. Also it delivers it promptly and with courtesy.

Believe it or not, company income and payroll depend upon *which* of the above four exchanges is in practice by (a) the company or (b) the employee.

If #1, "rip-off", is in vogue, income will dry up with a thoroughness you wouldn't believe. Although the TV and movies try to tell one that robbery is the only way to get rich, this is not true. Those who engage upon it, whether they be armed thieves or corporate con men, are not long for this world. The bigger the group, the longer it takes for it to fall, but fall it assuredly does. And the individual who takes, but does not give, ends up with a deep-six[1] in many ways quite rapidly.

The second condition of "partial exchange" can only keep a group or individual going just so long. The end result is painfully a demise of status or position and, most certainly, income. Many "Third World countries"[2] and even the bigger ones are in this plight right now. They take in, but do not really produce or give. This is what inflation is all about. The unemployment ranks are full of such people.

The third condition of "fair exchange" gives one a rather level progress. It is considered "honest", is socially acceptable and very legal. It does not, however, guarantee any expansion or improvement of a group or the lot of a person. It is barely comfortable.

The fourth condition is the preferred one. Produce in abundance and try to give better than expected quality. Deliver and get paid for it, for sure, but deliver better than was ordered and more. Always try to deliver a better job than was ordered. Always try to—and deliver—a better result than was hoped for.

This fourth principle above is almost unknown in business or the arts. Yet it is the key to howling success and expansion. It is true for the company; it is true for the individual employee.

Where a group is concerned, there is another factor that determines which of the four above is in practice. It is group *internal* pressure. Where this only comes from executives, it may not get activated. Where it comes from individual group members in the group itself, it becomes assured. The internal demand of one employee to another is what really determines the condition of the group and establishes which of the four conditions above come into play.

Thus the company collectively, in electing which of the four principles above it is following, establishes its own level of income and longevity and determines its own state of contraction or expansion.

While this is a must in an executive—to establish the principle being followed—the *real* manifestation only occurs from pressure by individual employees.

It is up to the individual employee what the company income is and what his own pay is. The company cannot earn more, and the individual employee cannot be paid more, than will be established by which principle above they elect to follow.

If they follow number 3, they will get along. But if they follow number 4, they will really flourish and prosper—*and* it is the only one which guarantees expansion.

---

[1] **deep-six:** (*idiom*) a discarding or disposing of something. To *"end up with a **deep-six**"* means to *end up being discarded or disposed of*. [This is a nautical expression indicating a water depth of 6 fathoms (36 feet); **deep-six** acquired its idiomatic definition from the fact that something thrown overboard at or greater than this depth would be difficult, if not impossible, to recover.]

[2] **Third World countries:** The term **"Third World"** refers to those countries, mostly former colonies that maintained their independence, that are not politically aligned with the West (the industrialized capitalist world, the "First World") or with the former Soviet Union and its allies (the "Second World"). However, the term can be misleading and, consequently, it has outlived its usefulness. It suggests a uniformity among countries that are extremely varied economically as well as culturally, socially and politically. They all share an objection to colonization and to foreign domination generally, but they hardly constitute a cohesive political force. The only characteristic common in all **Third World countries** is that their governments demand and receive Western aid. Today, the countries of the **Third World** are more commonly referred to as "developing countries". A developing country is a country that has low standards of democratic governments, industrialization, social programs and human rights guarantees that are yet to develop to those standards met in the West.

The Use of Statistics

Chapter 11

THE CONDITIONS:
Non-Existence and Above

The *declaration* of a Condition is something new. The Conditions, themselves, are not. Organizationally, a Condition is an operating state and, oddly enough, in the physical universe there is a formula[1] connected with each one of these operating states. One has to *do* the steps of a Condition formula in order to improve one's condition. These formulas apparently have to be followed in this universe or you go "appetite over tin cup".[2]

So one in his own personal life, in his operation of a job, the state of an organization, a family, a civilization, and the planet — all these will come under the heading of the Conditions and if they are in one Condition and operating on the formula of another, they for sure will fail.

It is a wonderful fact that these things exist and that they do regulate existence, regulate life, and that life can therefore be lived successfully by their use.

The different Conditions formulas make up a SCALE which shows the Condition or operating state, which is to say the degree of success or survival, of that individual job position, department, division or organization at any one particular time and as compared to other times.

Conditions from Non-Existence through Power are declared on the basis of *statistics*. A statistic is a number or amount *compared* to an earlier number or amount of the same thing. *Statistics* refer to the quantity of work done or the value of it in money. Statistics are the only sound measure of any production or any job or any activity. These tell of production. They measure what is done. And when one does the steps of the appropriate Condition formula, those actions will bring about a changed condition and will then be reflected in one's statistic.

SCALE OF CONDITIONS

Power Change

Power
Affluence
Normal Operation
Emergency
Danger
Non-Existence

Liability
Doubt

---

[1] **formula:** In general, a prescribed form or rule; a fixed or conventional method in which anything is to be done, arranged or said.

[2] **appetite over tin cup:** (*American slang*) a pioneer Western U.S. term used by riverboat men on the Missouri. It means thrown away violently, like *"head over heels"* (tumbling as if in a somersault), *"bowled over"* (astonished and confused).

Therefore, organizationally speaking, one has to be able to get a statistic on anything anywhere in the operation. If he can't, it's all on rumor and who knows what else, and he very soon will be in trouble.

We will discuss the Conditions of Non-Existence up through Power first. Then we will cover the Conditions that are not determined by one's own statistic: Power Change, which occurs when a person assumes a job position that has been successfully held by his predecessor, and then, in the next chapter, *Liability* and *Doubt*, which are Conditions below Non-Existence.

NON-EXISTENCE

There are only two circumstances when an employee would be in a Condition of Non-Existence:

1. **New Job Non-Existence.** Every new appointee to a job position, whether obtained by new appointment, promotion or demotion, begins in a Condition of Non-Existence because he has not yet produced anything in that capacity. He is normally under the delusion that now he is "THE _____" (new title). He tries to start off in Power Condition, as he is usually very aware of his new status or even a former status. But in actual fact *he* is the only one aware of it. All others except perhaps the Personnel Director are utterly unaware of him as having his new status. Therefore he begins in a state of Non-Existence. And if he does not begin with the Non-Existence Formula as his guide, he will be using the wrong Condition and will have all kinds of trouble.

2. **Non-Existence by statistics**. When one finds his statistic in such a low range that it shows no real products are being achieved, or those that are being worked on are moving so slowly that the activity is nonviable, he is in a Condition of Non-Existence.

In either of the above circumstances, one would apply the Non-Existence Formula:

> **NON-EXISTENCE FORMULA**
>
> 1. Find a communication line.
> 2. Make yourself known.
> 3. Discover what is needed or wanted.
> 4. Do, produce and/or present it.

Many employees misapply the Non-Existence Formula, whether for a new position or by statistics, and then wonder why they seem to continue in trouble. Because they misapplied or never really did the Non-Existence Formula on their jobs, they never came out of Non-Existence.

For example, the phrase "find a communication line" (Step 1) is shortened down by too many people to: locating somebody's in-basket and dropping in it a short memo asking the person, *"What is needed and wanted?"* (Step 3). This is not really finding a communication line. It is the duty of any employee, new on the job or not, *to round up the communication lines that relate to his job position, find out who needs vital information from him* and *get those lines in — in — in* as a continuing action. When a person fails to do just that, he never comes out of Non-Existence.

When one finds himself remaining in a Condition of Non-Existence for an extended period (a good rule to follow is that one should be in a Normal Condition within 30 days), he must apply the Expanded Non-Existence Formula:

EXPANDED NON-EXISTENCE FORMULA

1. Find and get yourself on every comm line you will need in order to give and obtain information relating to your duties and materiel.[3]

2. Make yourself known, along with your job title and duties, to every terminal you will need for the obtaining of information and the giving of data.

3. Discover from your seniors and fellow employees and any public your duties may require you to contact, what is needed and wanted from each.

4. Do, produce and present what each needs and wants that is in conformation with policy.

5. Maintain your comm lines that you have and expand them to obtain other information you now find you need on a routine basis.

6. Maintain your origination lines (originate the appropriate communication and follow up) to inform others what you are doing exactly, but only those who actually need the information.

7. Streamline what you are doing, producing and presenting so that it is more closely what is really needed and wanted.

8. With full information being given and received concerning your products, do, produce and present a greatly improved product routinely in your assigned area of responsibility and action.

---

[3] **materiel:** all the apparatus, equipment, parts and supplies (as distinguished from the personnel) required in an operation, organization or undertaking.

DANGER

A Danger Condition is normally assigned when:

a. An Emergency Condition has continued too long

b. A statistic plunges downward very steeply

c. A senior executive suddenly finds himself or herself wearing the hat of head of the activity because it is in trouble.

The usual action in an organization is to let things run, as long as they run well. When they begin to show poorer statistics, an Emergency Condition is assigned. If the Condition continues, the person in charge of the activity receives a warning. (In a continued Emergency Condition, it will always be found that noncompliance with policy and orders has for some time existed. It will sometimes be found that lies and false reports also existed. And one always finds negligence and idleness and inattention where statistics continue to go down.)

And if the statistics still go down, the usual course of action is to transfer or fire the person in charge and find somebody else. At the point where a senior executive finds he is being made to look bad by continued Emergency on a lower echelon,[4] he has no choice but to assign a Danger Condition. A continued Emergency inevitably results in real catastrophe for higher executives. It causes them heavy overwork at the very least. Sometimes a Danger Condition threatens, finally, the whole organization, unless handled.

The **Danger Formula** is the formula an executive, himself, applies when he assigns a junior or area under his control a Condition of Danger.

DANGER FORMULA

1. Bypass (ignore the junior or juniors normally in charge of the activity and handle it personally).

2. Handle the situation and any danger in it.

3. Assign the area where it had to be handled a Danger Condition.

4. Assign each individual connected with the Danger Condition a First Dynamic[5] Danger Condition and enforce and ensure that they follow the formula completely, and if they do not do so, do a full investigation and take all actions indicated.

5. Reorganize the activity so that the situation does not repeat.

6. Recommend any firm policy that will hereafter detect and/or prevent the Condition from recurring.

---

[4] **echelon:** one of a series of levels or grades in an organization or field of activity. (As used in the context above, a lower **echelon** is any level below that of the aforementioned senior executive.)

[5] **First Dynamic:** the urge toward survival as one's self. Here we have individuality expressed fully.

It is *very* bad to assign a Danger Condition or to bypass *unless* the statistics are continuing to go down or have continued at a dangerous level for some time without real improvement.

The **First Dynamic Danger Formula** is the formula one applies when his personal statistic is in a Danger Condition (per items "a" and "b" on the previous page). One would also apply this formula when he is assigned a Danger Condition by a senior executive (per item "c" on the previous page) because he had to be bypassed and his work had to be done for him or had to be continually corrected.

> **FIRST DYNAMIC DANGER FORMULA**
>
> 1. Bypass habits or normal routines.
>
> 2. Handle the situation and any danger in it.
>
> 3. Assign yourself a Danger Condition.
>
> 4. Get in your own *personal ethics*[6] by finding what you are doing that is out-ethics[7] and use self-discipline to correct it and get honest and straight.
>
> 5. Reorganize your life so that the dangerous situation is not continually happening to you.
>
> 6. Formulate and adopt firm policy that will hereafter detect and prevent the same situation from continuing to occur.

When production has again increased, the Danger Condition should be formally ended and an Emergency Condition assigned and its formula should be followed.

EMERGENCY

One applies the Condition of Emergency when:

1. Statistics of an organization or portion of an organization or a person are seen to be *declining*, or

2. Statistics of an organization or a portion of an organization or a person are *unchanging*.

Regarding point #2 above, it might seem, at first glance, that an *unchanging* statistic is a *stable condition* and, therefore, viable. After all, though the stat did not increase, it did not decrease either. So what would be wrong with striving to maintain the exact same production level week after week anyway?

---

[6] **personal ethics:** the rules or standards governing the conduct of a person. To *"get in one's own **personal ethics**"* means to abide by the rules or standards one has set for himself to achieve optimum survival.

[7] **out-ethics: 1.** an action or situation in which an individual is involved that is contrary to the ideals and best interests of his group. **2.** an act or situation or relationship that is contrary to the ethics standards, codes or ideals of the group or other members of the group. **3.** an act of omission or commission by an individual that could or has reduced the general effectiveness of a group or its other members. **4.** an individual act of omission or commission which impedes the general well-being of a group or impedes it in achieving its goals.

Actually, one cannot have a condition where there is no increase and no decrease. That's a totally stable condition and there is no such thing in this universe. There isn't anything that always remains the same. You cannot have a total, even state of existence which does not eventually fall on its head. The second you get this even state, it starts to deteriorate.

So, an *unchanging* statistic is not stable. It signifies a Condition of Emergency.

> **EMERGENCY FORMULA**
>
> 1. Promote.
>
>   That applies to an organization. To an individual you had better say, "produce". That's the first action regardless of any other action, regardless of anything else.
>
>   That is the first thing one has to put his attention on.
>
>   Exactly what is *promotion*? It is making things known. It is getting things out. It is getting oneself known, getting one's products out.
>
> 2. Change your operating basis.
>
>   If, for instance, you went into a Condition of Emergency and then you didn't change your operation after you had promoted, you will just head for another Condition of Emergency. So that has to be part of it. You had better change your operating basis because that operating basis led you into an Emergency.
>
> 3. Economize.
>
> 4. Prepare to deliver.
>
> 5. Stiffen discipline.
>
>   Part of the Condition of Emergency contains this little line of "you have got to stiffen discipline" or "you have got to stiffen ethics."
>
>   This would simply mean, for example, to not go down to the pub every Friday night. Stiffen up the discipline. Stay home and burn the midnight oil, do one's homework, etc. Be a little more regular on the job, work a little harder, don't goof quite so much, don't make so many mistakes. All of this would be part of stiffening discipline.

NORMAL OPERATION

You could call Normal a "condition of stability" and it probably should be called a condition of stability [meaning resistant to change, especially sudden change or deterioration]. However, as stated above, one cannot have a condition where there is no increase and no decrease. That's a totally stable condition and there is no such thing in this universe. The second you get this even state, it starts to deteriorate.

To prevent a deterioration, you must have an increase. The Condition of Normal Operation, then, is not one of "stability". Normal Operation must be a routine or gradual increase. That increase doesn't have to be spectacular but it has to be something. There has to be a bit of an increase there.

> **NORMAL FORMULA**
>
> 1. Don't change anything. The way you maintain an increase is, when you are in a state of Normal Operation, you don't change anything.
>
> 2. Ethics are very mild. The justice factor is quite mild and quite reasonable. There are no savage actions taken particularly.
>
> 3. Every time a statistic betters, look it over carefully and find out *what* bettered it. And then do that without abandoning what you were doing before. Those are the only changes you make.
>
> 4. Every time a statistic worsens slightly, quickly find out *why* and remedy it.
>
> And you just jockey[8] those two factors: the statistic bettering, the statistic worsening. You will find out, inevitably, some change has been made in that area where a statistic worsens. Some *change* has been made and you better get that change off the lines[9] in a hurry. And when you find that a statistic is bettering, you better find out *how* it is bettering.

AFFLUENCE

When you have a line going steeply up on a statistic graph[10], that's Affluence. Whether it's up steeply for one week or up steeply from its last point week after week after week, it's Affluence.

When you've got an Affluence, regardless of how you did it, the Affluence Formula applies.

You *must* apply the Affluence Formula or you will be in trouble. Anyone dealing with Affluence should be aware of the following peculiarities about it.

Affluence is the most touchy Condition there is. Misname it or misapply the formula and it can destroy you! It is, strangely enough, the most dangerous of all Conditions in that if you don't spot it and apply the formula, you spatter all over the street! Spot and handle it right and it's a rocket ride.

---

[8] **jockey:** to direct or maneuver (something) by skill for one's advantage.

[9] **get that change off the lines:** a **line** is a route along which a particle travels between one terminal and the next in an organization; it is a fixed pattern of terminals who originate and receive, or receive and relay, orders, information or other particles. Particles such as orders, information and products "flow" or move along the **lines** in an organization. Sometimes, a change in policy or procedure can occur that consequently worsens the statistic in an area. Once discovered, one must **"get that change off the lines"**, i.e., revert to the earlier policy or operating basis, in order to improve the statistic.

[10] **graph:** a line or diagram showing how one quantity depends on, compares with or changes another. It is any pictorial device used to display numerical relationships.

> **AFFLUENCE FORMULA**
>
> The Affluence Formula for *finance* is:
>
> 1. Economize. Now the first thing you must do in Affluence is economize and then make very, very sure that you don't buy anything that has any future commitment to it. Don't buy anything with any future commitments; don't hire anybody with any future commitments—nothing. That is all part of that economy. Clamp it down.
>
> 2. Pay every bill. Get every bill that you can possibly scrape up from anyplace, every penny you owe anywhere under the sun, moon and stars and pay them. Pull everything down in all directions until you have got it down to *as close to* zero as you can get, or *at* zero.
>
> 3. Invest the remainder in service facilities.[11] Make it more possible to deliver.
>
> 4. Discover what *caused* the Condition of Affluence and strengthen it.

The Affluence Formula, which is applicable to *finances*, is modified to address the *actions* of an individual, unit, section, etc., within an organization. When those *actions* result in an Affluence Condition, based on statistical measurement, one would apply the *Action Affluence Formula*.

> **ACTION AFFLUENCE FORMULA**
>
> 1. *Economize* on needless or dispersed actions that did not contribute to the present Condition. Economize financially by knocking off all *waste*.
>
> 2. Make every action count and don't engage in any useless actions. Every new action to contribute and be of the same kind as *did* contribute.
>
> 3. Consolidate all gains. Any place we have gotten a gain, we keep it. Don't let things relax or go downhill or roller coaster.[12] Any advantage or gain we have, keep it, maintain it.
>
> 4. Discover for yourself what *caused* the Condition of Affluence in your immediate area and strengthen it.

---

[11] **service facilities:** **Facilities** are things that make an action, operation or course of conduct easier. When a senior executive has the ability to make money for the organization or greatly raise statistics, and when this ability has been demonstrated, that executive should have **facilities**. They normally include those things that unburden lines, speed lines, gather data, compile, buy leisure, defend, and extend longevity on the job. A **service facility** is simply a person, such as an assistant, or an item of equipment that facilitates an executive's ability to provide more, better or faster service.

[12] **roller coaster:** (*verb*) to move steeply up and down; to rise and fall like a **roller coaster** ride.

POWER

A Power stat is a stat in a very high range; a brand-new range in a Normal trend.[13] A Power stat is not just a stat that is steeply up for a long time. Nor is Power simply a very high stat. Power is not a one-week thing. Power is a *trend*.

DEFINITION: Power is a Normal in a stellar range so high that it is total abundance, no doubt about it. It is a stat that has gone up into a whole new, steeply high range and maintained that range; and now, in that new high range, it is on a Normal trend.

Operating in this new range, you may get a slight dip in that stat now and then. But it is still Power.

There is another datum that is of importance if one is to correctly recognize and understand this Condition: Why do we call it Power? BECAUSE THERE IS SUCH AN ABUNDANCE OF PRODUCTION THERE THAT MOMENTARY HALTS OR DIPS CAN'T PULL IT DOWN OR IMPERIL ITS SURVIVAL.

And *that* is *Power*. Of course, a person can only work so many hours in a day. He can only get so much individual production in a day. But he can get enough production in a day to support himself. He can get his production up into such abundance that he can take some time off. That depends on his efficiency and brightness.

The question would be "How much work can one person do?" Or "How many bricks can someone lay in a day?" At a certain peak of Affluence he will hit how many bricks he can lay. By increasing practice and efficiency, he can keep that level of production going in a Normal. If he's laying so many bricks that nobody is ever going to think of firing him, then he's in Power. That's a Power Condition for an individual.

POWER FORMULA

1. Don't disconnect.

   The first law of a Condition of Power is *don't disconnect*. That will bring about catastrophe for both you and anybody else. You can't just deny your connections. What you've got to do is take *ownership* and *responsibility* for your connections.

2. Write up the hat for your job position.

   The first thing you have to do is write up your entire hat (which includes the purpose and product of your position, as well as its relative location on the organizing board). Make a record of all of your job position's lines. By writing up your hat, you make it possible for the next fellow to assume the state of Power Change —of *changing nothing*—because you've shown what was there so he knows what *not* to change.

   So your *responsibility* is to write up your hat and get it into the hands of the person who is going to take care of it. Do all you can to make the job position occupiable. Sooner or later somebody is going to come along and occupy it properly.

---

[13] **trend:** an inclination toward a general course or direction.

POWER CHANGE

Unlike the Condition of Power, where the person himself goes into a Condition of Power, the Condition of Power Change is actually a person assuming a Condition that has been held from Power by someone else.

For example, you're replacing Bill, who was in a Condition of Power. Now, when he moves off, you, the one who took over, are the *Power Change*.

Another example would be where a company is running all right, but the general manager has been hired by some other company because he has such a successful record, and his job is taken over. The person who replaces him is the *Power Change*.

Correctly applying the formula for the Condition of Power Change makes it possible for a person to successfully take over a job his predecessor left behind.

POWER CHANGE FORMULA

When taking over a new job position, change nothing until you are thoroughly familiar with your new zone of power.

There is nothing to it; just step in the successful pair of boots you inherited and don't bother to walk. If the job position was in a Normal State of Operation, which it most likely would have been in for anybody to have been promoted out of it, you just *don't change anything*.

You just sit around for a while and observe. Learn the new job position before doing anything. Study the organization, policies, lines, patterns and activity. Go through the exact same routine of every day that your predecessor went through; sign nothing that he wouldn't sign; don't change a single order. Look through the papers that have been issued—these are the orders that are extant—and get busy just enforcing those orders. *Issue no orders* that are not routine—change nothing, innovate nothing. Keep your eyes open, learn the ropes, and depending on how big the organization is, after a certain time, see how it's running and, if it's not in any Condition other than a Normal Operating Condition, just apply the Normal Condition Formula to it. Besides doing the little routine of *"don't change anything"* (Step 1 of the Normal Condition Formula), go around and snoop around and find out what made it a little bit better that week and reinforce that (Step 3 of the Normal Condition Formula). And find out what worsened a little bit and take that out (Step 4 of the Normal Condition Formula). Just sniff around. By that time, you're so well acquainted with the operation, you know everyone by his first and last names; you know this, that and the other thing; you know where all the papers are; you know the favorite dodges[14] and you've seen all these things happen and, frankly, the operation will just keep on moving up. It will move ahead very successfully.

---

[14] **dodge:** (*noun*) an expedient; something contrived or used to meet an urgent need. [Example: *During the annual product inventory, rather than counting each item in accordance with company policy, Joe would use his favorite* **dodge** *of counting stacks of products, making the assumption that each stack contained 50 units.*]

CORRECT DESIGNATION OF CONDITIONS

There is a law that holds true in this universe whereby if one does not correctly designate the Condition he is in and apply its formula to his activities, or if he assigns and applies the wrong Condition, then the following happens: He will inevitably drop one Condition below the Condition he is *actually* in. Thus, if one incorrectly says he is in Power and tries to apply that formula when he is *actually* in Normal, he will inevitably drop to Emergency. If one incorrectly states he is in Normal when he is *actually* in Emergency, he will drop to Danger. Therefore, it is vital to accurately and honestly ascertain the Condition one is in and apply that formula and actually do it. Otherwise, one can go the route of applying the wrong formula and he'll drop down the Conditions without ever understanding why. Whole nations do this and it is one of the reasons for the decline of civilizations. And while one is not a nation, one is still important enough to properly handle Conditions. And remember that it is not enough to do this as a simple administrative exercise; one actually has to *do* the formulas if he ever expects his condition to improve.

ASSUMING JOB POSITIONS

There are just four circumstances one encounters when assuming a job position:

1. Assuming a NEW job position, never before occupied
2. Taking over a going concern,[15] a position that someone has successfully occupied
3. Taking over a job position from someone who has unsuccessfully occupied it
4. Taking over a collapsed job position, i.e., a completely failed position, no longer occupied.

NEW POSITIONS

One takes over a *new* job position in Non-Existence. He would apply the Non-Existence Formula.

SUCCESSFUL REPLACEMENTS

One takes over a going concern by the Power Change Formula.

UNSUCCESSFUL REPLACEMENTS

For the fellow who walks into the boots of somebody who has left in disgrace — the statistics have crashed causing that person to be fired — all he's got to do when he inherits a position with crashed statistics is nothing extraordinary. It's just apply the Emergency Formula to it, which is to *immediately produce!* (For the person who replaces the head of an organization, his first step in the Emergency Formula would be to *promote*.)

---

[15] **going concern:** a business or job position that is operating successfully and is likely to continue to do so.

Example: Eve was ranked the top sales rep in her company for the past several years. Her track record in product sales is legendary. However, Fred, the sales manager, just learned that during the past several months, Eve had routinely made unauthorized money-back guarantees to her customers. Ultimately, the company was obligated to refund nearly $85,000 to the customers to whom Eve made guarantees that could not be honored. In addition, other customers filed lawsuits. Eve was immediately terminated; she left in disgrace. Fred hired Steve, a salesman with an impressive sales record, to replace her. Assessing the situation upon his arrival, Steve assumed that he should apply the Danger Formula because the statistic of the job he took over was in Danger. He quickly learned that doing so was incorrect. Upon reading the Danger Formula, he concluded that he couldn't possibly apply it to a position he never held before. He clearly saw this on the very first step, *"Bypass habits or normal routines."* As a new arrival to the position, he had no *habits* or *routines* to bypass. Also, Step 4, *"Get in your own **personal ethics** by finding what you are doing that is out-ethics…"* did not apply, as he had just taken over the position and hadn't done anything to cause the Danger. As he looked over the Conditions formulas, Steve realized that the correct Condition formula to apply when replacing someone whose stats have crashed is the Emergency Condition Formula. He needed to immediately *"produce"* (Step 1).

COLLAPSED POSITIONS

One takes over a collapsed job position in Non-Existence. He would apply the Non-Existence Formula.

Example: Warren owns a physical therapy practice. Several years ago, he had a billing clerk, Rachel, whom he never supervised closely. During a three-month period, she lost more than $60,000 in accounts receivable. She failed to bill hundreds of claims, she forgave patient debt without Warren's knowledge or permission and much of what she did submit to insurance companies for payment was rejected due to her coding errors. On top of all that, she embezzled more than five thousand dollars in cash paid by patients. By the time Warren learned of Rachel's unscrupulous activities, the billing department was in shambles. Warren fired Rachel immediately. However, he had no time to sort out the area, so he hired an outside company to do all his billing and collections from that day forward. For the past three years he has noticed a steady decline in the percentage collected from what was billed. Warren decided to bring billing and collections back in-house. He hired Judy to re-establish the collapsed billing department. As she did not take over the position directly from Rachel (which would have necessitated application of the Emergency Formula in such circumstances), Judy applied the Non-Existence Formula to her new position.

AFFLUENCE ATTAINMENT

In order to achieve the Affluence Condition, one must consider five key factors, one of which is, of course, the correct application of the formula for the Condition he is in. Regardless of whether one's job statistic is in the Condition of Non-Existence, Danger, Emergency or Normal, if he desires to attain the Condition of Affluence, he should always strive to implement the following components in the daily performance of his job.

AFFLUENCE ATTAINMENT

Affluence Attainment consists of:

1. HARD WORK

By *hard work* we do not mean work that is oppressive or backbreaking to do. Rather, it is work that is performed with or marked by great diligence or energy. To attain Affluence, the first step, then, is to work hard—to apply oneself thoroughly to the job, to persevere through any stops or barriers one might encounter and to approach work that way each and every day.

2. IN-ETHICS

The dictionary defines *ethics* as "the rules or standards governing the conduct of a person or the conduct of the members of a profession." ETHICS are the actions an individual takes on himself in order to accomplish optimum survival for himself and others on all dynamics. It is a personal thing. It is a First Dynamic action. When one is ethical or *has his ethics in*, it is by his own determination. He himself takes the actions to be ethical. In other words, he puts his own ethics in; he and his actions are said to be *in-ethics*.

3. *STANDARD* TECH

When it comes to scientific or mechanical processes, the right ways to do things are called TECHNICAL PROCEDURES or TECH. There is a TECH of ADMIN; this would be the right ways to do administrative actions or organize something. For any type of work one does, the proper way to do it is called "technical procedure" or TECH. Unvarying adherence to the precise technical procedures of one's job is called **STANDARD TECH.**

4. DOING THE THINGS THAT *WON*, NOT NEW THINGS UNTRIED AS YET

The things that won would be those actions one has taken previously in the course of his work that have produced consistently good results. If something one has done worked well, then it stands to reason that repeating that same winning action would continue to bring about success. On the other hand, doing something that has not yet been tried, instead of adhering to a proven winning action, could be disastrous.

NOTE: This step in Affluence Attainment does NOT mean that one would never try something new to improve the company. Organizations routinely implement new ideas, procedures and products. However, there's a lot of trial and error that occurs in developing a new way of doing business. That's why a new program should be administered only as a "special project" for a while, off the company's main lines, under special management. When a special project is seen to be effective or, especially, profitable, it is then put into the organization lines as a successful action, as a *thing that won*.

5. APPLYING THE FORMULA OF THE CONDITION ONE IS IN

Chapter 12

THE CONDITIONS:
BELOW NON-EXISTENCE

There are five Conditions, or operating states, below the level of Non-Existence, that cannot be determined from the slant of a line on a graph. When one goes into a Condition below Non-Existence, he must apply the formula of that Condition and then move up each Condition in sequence by completing the formulas for those Conditions until he arrives once again to the Condition that is reflected in his statistic.

We will address only the first two Conditions below Non-Existence, as it is not uncommon to encounter them in the course of doing business. Knowing and applying their formulas can get an employee successfully through two of the toughest situations he might experience at work: (1) when he has knowingly caused damage or (2) when he can't decide if he even wants to keep his job.

LIABILITY

Below Non-Existence there is the Condition of Liability. The person has ceased to be simply nonexistent as a team member and has taken on the color[1] of an enemy. It is assigned where careless or malicious and knowing damage is caused to projects, organizations or activities. It is adjudicated that it is malicious and knowing because orders have been published against it or because it is contrary to the intentions and actions of the remainder of the team or the purpose of the project or organization.

It is a *liability* to have such a person unwatched as the person may do or continue to do things to stop or impede the forward progress of the project or organization and such a person cannot be trusted. No discipline or the assignment of Conditions above it has been of any avail. The person has just kept on messing up.

The Condition is usually assigned when several Dangers and Non-Existences have been assigned or when a long unchanged pattern of conduct has been detected. When all others are looking for the reason mail is getting lost, such a person would keep on losing the mail covertly.

The Condition is assigned for the benefit of others so they won't get tripped up trusting the person in any way.

---

[1] **color:** character or nature. Often used in the plural. [Example: *revealed their true* **colors**]

> **LIABILITY FORMULA**
>
> 1. Decide who are one's friends.
>
> 2. Deliver an effective blow to the enemies of the group one has been pretending to be part of, despite personal danger.
>
> 3. Make up the damage one has done by personal contribution far beyond the ordinary demands of a group member.
>
> 4. Apply for reentry to the group by asking the permission of each member of it to rejoin, and rejoining only by majority permission; and if refused, repeating (2) and (3) and (4) until one is allowed to be a group member again.

DOUBT

When one cannot make up one's mind as to an individual, a group, organization or project, a Condition of Doubt exists.

> **DOUBT FORMULA**
>
> 1. Inform oneself honestly of the actual intentions and activities of that individual, group, project or organization, brushing aside all bias and rumor.
>
> 2. Examine the statistics of the individual, group, project or organization.
>
> 3. Decide on the basis of "the greatest good for the greatest number of dynamics" whether or not it should be attacked, harmed, suppressed or helped.
>
> 4. Evaluate oneself or one's own group, project or organization as to intentions and objectives.
>
> 5. Evaluate one's own statistics or one's group's, project's or organization's statistics.
>
> 6. Join or remain in or befriend the one which progresses toward the greatest good for the greatest number of dynamics and announce the fact publicly to both sides.
>
> 7. Do everything possible to improve the actions and statistics of the person, group, project or organization one has remained in or joined.
>
> 8. Suffer on up through the Conditions in the new group if one has changed sides, or the Conditions of the group one has remained in if wavering from it has lowered one's status.

Example: Sam works as an insurance salesman at Mathis & Associates, a small brokerage firm. He has been complaining to a friend that he's not completely satisfied with his job. His pay hasn't increased much in the past couple of years and he sometimes feels like he's not appreciated. His friend, Kevin, told him about Apperson Insurance Group, a rival brokerage firm that is hiring agents. Kevin once worked there and had nothing but great things to say about his experience. So Sam scheduled a job interview to find out more about the position being offered. He met with Roy, the sales manager, who told Sam all about the company's big plans to become the premier provider of employment insurance to small businesses throughout the county. Roy told Sam he could easily earn a six-figure income and that, with his experience, he would be perfect for the job. Sam, who is only earning a high five-figure income at Mathis, was very interested. He also noted that the Apperson office is much closer to his home than Mathis. It would cut off at least 20 minutes each way from his commute. He took a brief tour of the office and noticed a few things that concerned him: (1) the statistics posted in the boardroom were mostly down-trending, (2) he overheard a couple of employees talking about how high the personnel turnover is and that several people have just been laid off, and (3) he noticed that several people sitting at their desks seemed stressed or unhappy. By the time he left the firm, Sam couldn't make up his mind about what he should do. So, when he got home that evening, he decided to do the formula for the Condition of Doubt. He wrote the following:

DOUBT FORMULA

1. **Inform myself honestly of the actual intentions and activities of that organization (Apperson), brushing aside all bias and rumor.**

   I've heard rumors that the company has a high turnover rate and that people are being laid off. Kevin is highly biased in favor of the company. I felt comfortable with the management,[2] but wasn't impressed with some of the staff that I met. Brushing all that aside, what I KNOW is that the Apperson Insurance Group's actual intentions are admirable. They want to expand their organization and help businesses in their community. They appear to operate in an ethical manner, as I have confirmed that no one has filed a single complaint against them in the past five years.

2. **Examine the statistics of the organization (Apperson).**

   Apperson's stats are disappointing. I saw that their gross income has been down-trending for the past six months. I also saw that the number of staff has dropped by about 15% in that same period. So, it appears the company is in a state of contraction, not expansion.

3. **Decide on the basis of what would be the greatest good for the greatest number of dynamics whether or not it (Apperson) should be attacked, harmed, suppressed or helped.**

   If I were to go to work for Apperson, I would have more time to spend with my family (2nd Dynamic), as I would save time going to and from work. My health club is right around the corner from the office, so I could work out during my lunch break (1st Dynamic). I could definitely help the organization become less stressful and more stable with regard to its income (3rd Dynamic). From my limited knowledge of Apperson, I don't know

---

[2] **management:** the person or persons controlling or directing the affairs of a business, institution, organization, etc. [Example: *The store is under new* **management**.]

what impact, if any, my working there would have on the 4th through 8th Dynamics. Based on my assessment and what would be the greatest good for the greatest number of dynamics, Apperson should definitely be helped.

4. **Evaluate my own organization (Mathis) as to its intentions and objectives.**

   I've been with Mathis for eight years. For the past six years, the company has met or exceeded all its goals as stated in their annual strategic plans. Their mission statement includes putting the needs of the customer first, a policy that I fully support. Their objective is to form a cohesive group capable of managing steady growth, so as to bring about high employee retention and organizational stability.

5. **Evaluate my organization's (Mathis') statistics.**

   Mathis is doing very well. While they are a smaller company than Apperson, they have been growing steadily the entire time I've been with them. They promote from within by training staff to take on greater responsibilities. They always paid for any continuing education I have requested. My pay is not as high as I would like, but I could earn more if I take on additional responsibilities or increase my sales.

6. **Join or remain in or befriend the one which progresses toward the greatest good for the greatest number of dynamics and announce the fact publicly to both sides.**

   The company that progresses toward the greatest good for the greatest number of dynamics is Mathis. So I'm going to stay where I am. There are too many unknowns at Apperson at this time. While the immediate potential for higher income is there, I'm just not convinced that the company can sustain their planned growth. And, at the moment, they ARE declining. I like the people with whom I currently work (3rd and 7th Dynamics) and it is a stress-free environment. Apperson's staff seemed stressed out. I will be fully vested in the company's retirement plan in just two years, which will provide security for my family (2nd Dynamic) and me (1st Dynamic). At Apperson, I would be starting all over and their health care plan is not as good as the one I have at Mathis (1st and 2nd Dynamics). The 4th, 5th, 6th and 8th Dynamics don't have an impact on my decision regarding which job to take. I will call Apperson tomorrow and respectfully decline their offer. I will let my supervisor know that I am reaffirming my desire and intention to make Mathis my "home".

7. **Do everything possible to improve the actions and statistics of the organization I have remained in.**

   I will request a meeting with my supervisor to let him know that, on occasion, I've felt that he didn't adequately acknowledge or appreciate my hard work. I'll tell him I want to look at ways I can assume more responsibilities to increase my pay. I will take additional classes to make myself even more valuable to the company. Finally, I will take an active part in company staff meetings, where our suggestions are elicited.

8. **Suffer on up through the Conditions of the group I have remained in if wavering from it has lowered my status.**

   Looking at another job opportunity did not lower my status with Mathis. So there is no need to move up through Liability, Non-Existence, etc. I will continue to apply the Normal Condition formula as indicated by my VFP statistic.

Chapter 13

READING STATISTICS

Organizations operate on statistics. Stats show whether or not an employee or group is working or not working, as it is the work that produces the statistic. If one doesn't work effectively, the statistic inevitably goes down. If he works effectively, the statistic goes up.

One reads[1] a statistic to determine which of the Conditions formulas he needs to apply to either keep a statistic rising (if it is already going up) or halt its descent and get it going up (if it is falling). The weekly Condition assignments must be accurate. Only in that way can one maintain expansion. In weekly Condition assignments one only considers two things: that exact week and the slant of that one line.

In an organization, one reads the division statistics for the *week*. A department reads its statistics by the *day*. A section does it by the *hour*. One can also read all main divisional statistics by the day; successful organizations do.

The following are weekly statistic graphs that illustrate one week's worth of statistics. The description of the slant of the line and the appropriate Condition one would assign to it, assuming that the graphs are properly scaled, are provided.

Steep near vertical down:

NON-EXISTENCE

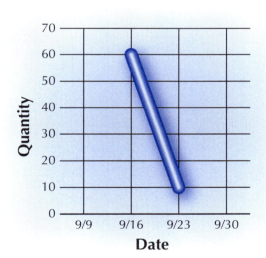

---

[1] **read:** to examine and grasp the meaning of a graphic representation.

Down:

DANGER

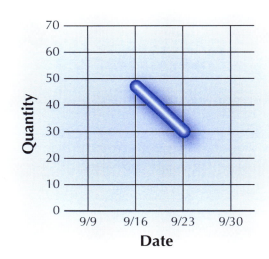

Slightly down or level:

EMERGENCY

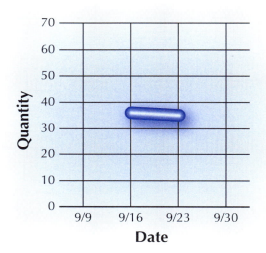

The volume of the stat has little to do with it. Level at high or level at low are alike Emergency.

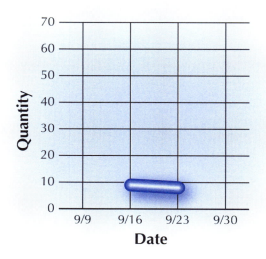

Slightly up:

NORMAL

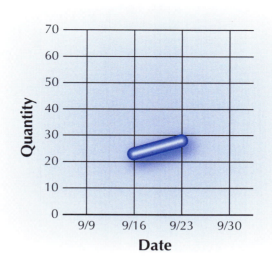

Steeply up:

AFFLUENCE

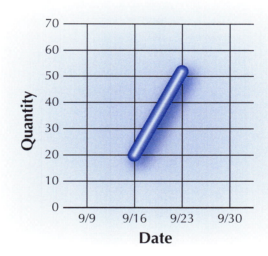

NOTE: (1) These slant lines illustrating Non-Existence through Affluence represent the statistic Condition *for the week*. If one graphs statistics *by the day* or *by the hour*, he could likewise apply the formula of the Condition indicated by the daily or hourly statistic, in order to bring about an increase in that statistic by the next day or hour, respectively. (2) While the Conditions of Non-Existence through Affluence can be determined by the slant of a single line on a graph, the Power Condition cannot. Power is determined *by trend* only. It must be determined by more than one week's worth of statistics.

UPSIDE DOWN GRAPHS

There is a technology to graphing statistics. This includes stats that should be graphed "upside down".

There are several ways to handle it, but a graph which, when it goes down, is good news and when it goes up is bad news has to be graphed differently than other graphs. Otherwise the wrong Conditions could be assigned to it.

One of the ways to handle this is to reverse the numbers on the left side of the graph so that zero is at the top. It is simply a matter of plotting the graph "upside down" so far as the numerical vertical scale on the left is concerned.

Example: Ellen works in Quality Control (QC) at a small manufacturing company. It is her job to investigate consumer complaints regarding defective products. One of the statistics by which she measures her production is the number of QC complaints received by the company each week. Graphed in the usual way, with zero at the bottom of the graph, a decrease in the number of complaints would be erroneously assigned a Condition of Emergency or below. However, if the statistic were graphed "upside down" (with zero at the top of the scale) then proper Conditions could be assigned to it. When such a graph goes up, it means that fewer complaints were received than the previous week and when it goes down, more complaints were received than the previous week. By graphing such a statistic "upside down", you will find that the Conditions formulas apply to it. With complaints graphed in this way one could gauge the effectiveness of quality control measures. It certainly doesn't become an Emergency Condition when the number of complaints received decreases.

Sample upside down graph:

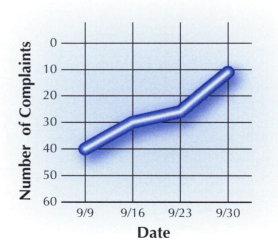

One must look and determine whether an increasing number or amount of something is good or bad. Examples of other stats that should be graphed "upside down" would be (1) the number or amount of refunds requested, (2) the amount of unpaid bills and (3) the number of hours of unauthorized employee absence. All of these are good news when decreasing. The vertical scale of any such stat graph should be reversed so that Conditions can be assigned to them properly.

One must realize that, in a statistic, one is handling an indicator of complex conditions and that stats are indicators of the real world. They are not things in themselves. It is vital to use stats and vital to use the Conditions formulas, but remember that a stat is simply an index of things as they have been and that stats inform you of the relative need of action and that the Condition formula is a tool to change (for the better) the future of the thing that the statistic represents.

COMPLETING CONDITIONS FORMULAS

The Conditions formulas flow, one to the next, with the first step of one formula directly following the final step of the previous (i.e., the next <u>lower</u> Condition) formula. And within each Condition formula, there is a flow from one step to the next step of that Condition formula. [See APPENDIX on page 163.]

But what do you do if your stat graph indicates you've moved up a Condition before you even have a chance to finish a formula? Do you just drop that formula and start on the next one? The answer is "NO". One completes the formula he has begun.

Example: Amanda is the front desk person at a dental practice. At the beginning of a new week, she looks over her VFP, "Scheduled Patients Arriving for Service", and sees that her weekly statistic, "Percentage of Arrivals", is in Emergency. Her percentage of arrivals was only 75% last week, when it was at 80% the previous week. She immediately begins to PRODUCE, Step 1 of the Emergency Formula, calling each patient to confirm his appointment. Once that is well in hand, she begins Step 2, CHANGE YOUR OPERATING BASIS. She gives appointment reminder cards to each patient upon departure and makes it a matter of routine to do all her confirmation calls first thing each morning. But before she has a chance to do each of the remaining steps of the Emergency Formula, her arrivals percentage statistic moves up into Normal Operation on Wednesday.

What does she do? Well, she's now in a Condition of Normal by stats. However, Amanda can get continued improvement on her graph by *completing* the Emergency Formula, as the actions on the Emergency Formula are what got her to Normal so quickly. Even the Normal Formula would also cause her to complete the Emergency Formula, because in the Normal Formula one drops out what is unsuccessful and he pushes what was successful; what was successful here was applying the Emergency Formula. So she would do the remaining steps of the Emergency Formula until they were fully completed. This doesn't mean that Amanda is still in an Emergency Condition—the stats are now rising and the Condition *is* Normal.

That one's stats rise before completing a formula doesn't mean he can't go into a higher Condition his stats now indicate. However, if undone steps of an earlier formula are not completed, one could soon find his stats down again. So, as in the above example, one has to complete the earlier formula, then complete the next formula and continue on as his graph indicates.

One will not always get a stat rise before he has a chance to fully complete a formula. But he had better make sure every step of each Condition formula is fully DONE.

Completing a formula is very vital. One doesn't just name a formula. He gets it *completed*.

RATIONALIZING STATISTICS

"Rationalizing a statistic" is a derogatory term meaning finding excuses for down-statistics. Finding excuses or reasons why a stat is down does NOT bring it up.

As stated previously, the weekly Condition assignments must be accurate. Only in that way can one maintain expansion.

Here is a typical argument about statistics: "I know it's down a bit, but it's so high generally, that it's Power." (Even with stats validly in a Power range, one would handle a dip in the stats with the appropriate Condition formula.) To discount a fall just because stats are high, high, high is folly. They *could* do week before last's, as they *did* it. So what was wrong that they couldn't do it again? If they got exhausted at it week before last, they need more help, obviously. Or better organization.

If down-statistics for the week are brushed off, the organization will shrink, become less stable, will demand more work by fewer and will be a burden.

Also, it's a bit mean to nag around about a rise. "But it isn't much of a rise; you're really in too low a range to have a rise count . . ." or "I know it rose, but it's so low that it's really Non-Existence." All this is being *reasonable*.[2] It indicates you don't value statistics. When you are being reasonable, you don't catch the improvements or flubs[3] that, piled up, wreck an organization. A rise is a rise. They at least got more. Now, with better organizing, they will get more than that. Week by week it goes up.

When you manage by the statistic, you don't go wrong. But it has to be an honest statistic, and explanations that aren't the real reason for rises and falls have to be rejected.

One can always make stats go up. Hard work. Foresight. Initiative. One can always make stats go up. That's the truth of it, and it needs no explanations.

USING JUDGMENT

In reading statistics, there is a factor known as judgment. There is no rote[4] method of determining the Condition of a stat by the number of degrees of angle from the horizontal. If the Condition of a stat is not immediately obvious (and it should be with a quick glance at the graph if it is drawn properly), then judgment is the key. One must realize that a Condition is an operating state of existence.

Some people do manage to apply judgment to their stats and their job positions when they have some kind of doubt as to what Condition to apply in order to resolve their stats and raise them.

---

[2] **reasonable:** accepting or tolerant of faulty explanations. Being **reasonable** is a symptom of being unable to recognize illogical data for what they are and being unable to use the data to discover actual situations.

[3] **flubs:** embarrassing, clumsy mistakes.

[4] **rote: 1.** (*noun*) a memorizing process using routine or repetition, often without full attention or comprehension. **2.** (*adj.*) learned or memorized **by rote. 3.** (*idiom*) **by rote**: from memory, without thought of the meaning; in a mechanical way. [Example: *to learn a language* **by rote**]

Example: Jeff is an insurance salesman. On a good week he sells twenty life insurance policies. Last week (10/21), he only sold ten policies and his statistic barely increased from the week before. Furthermore, for the previous three weeks, his statistics have steeply declined. [See graph below.] Jeff's statistic is in an unacceptable range for the amount of income he needs to generate. As he looked over his statistic, his inclination was to apply the Danger Formula because he felt he was *"in too low a range to have a rise count."* Fortunately, he realized he was being *reasonable*. After all, his stat *did* go up last week. So Jeff looked at the steps of the Conditions formulas to decide which formula would best handle the scene and raise his stat back up to the higher Conditions. **This is the factor of judgment.** Jeff thought to himself, *"How am I going to handle this scene and resolve the statistic that measures it? Well, let's see what Condition this is really in. Well, the stat **is** going up, and I'm sure that if I keep doing what I'm doing* [i.e., don't change anything] *I can get it up again. Hey, that's the Normal Formula… that's right… I'm in Normal! Okay. That's the Condition formula I will do."* So Jeff correctly applied the Normal Formula this week and, by the end of the week, his stats went up even further.

Basically, you must realize that one can go pretty rote on this and the real way to do it is to understand the Conditions formulas, understand what one is trying to do and what one is trying to get done, and apply the correct Condition formula. And only then will management by stats begin to work well for you. In this case, however, *trends* are very important.

STATISTIC TRENDS

The interpretation of statistics includes *trend*—meaning an inclination toward a general course or direction. Trends are used within a company to estimate expansion or warn of contraction.

As evident from the illustrations on pages 69-71, it is a simple action to determine the Condition of a stat on a one-week basis by looking at the slant of the one line for that week.

There is a bit more tech involved in determining the Condition of a stat by trend. To determine a stat trend, one needs to look at several weeks' worth of statistics.

The closer one is to the scene of the statistic, the smaller the amount of time is needed to interpret it and the easier it is to change it.

Example:

> ➢ One's own personal statistic can be graphed and interpreted hour to hour.

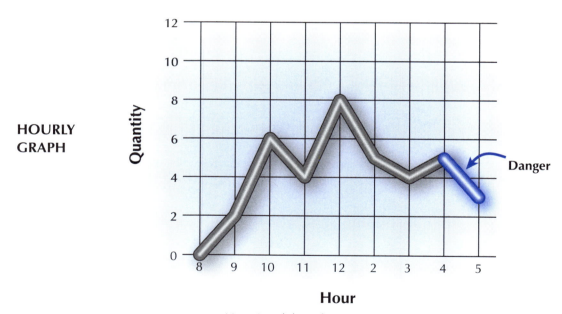

Note: Lunch hour from 12-1 is not reflected in the statistic or the horizontal scale.

➤ The statistic of a department's or division's VFP can be graphed and interpreted day to day.

DAILY GRAPH

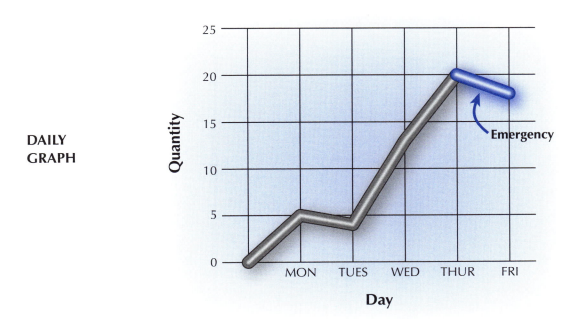

➤ An executive director or company president would use a week's worth of statistics.

WEEKLY GRAPH

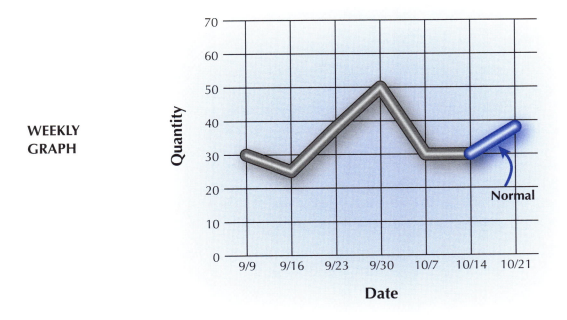

➤ A more remote governing body would interpret stats using a *trend*. A regional manager would use three weeks' worth of stats, whereas an executive in a remote management area, e.g., corporate headquarters, would use a period of six weeks.

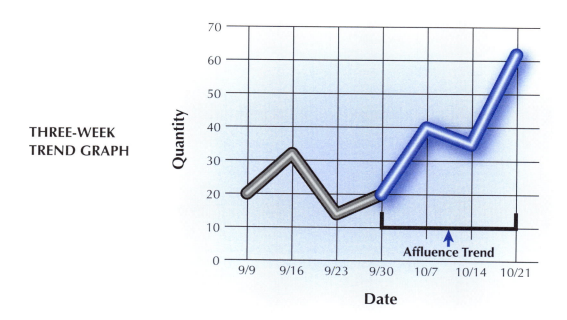

THREE-WEEK TREND GRAPH

Statistic *trends* are measured over a three- or six-week period or longer. *Trends* can be anything from Danger to Power, depending on the slant and its steepness. It is also possible to have a Non-Existence trend.

READING STAT TRENDS

Trends are not hard to read, but it is done with the EYE. There is no system of lines that can be drawn to assist this. One sits back and looks at the picture as a whole, and there is a definite slant one can determine by this action. You have to visually average the peaks and valleys. You look at the peaks and note the trend they are taking. You look at the valleys and note the trend they are taking. You then visually average the two trends and you will SEE the general direction, the trend, the stat is taking. Is it tilting slightly downward? Steeply downward? Is it level? Tilting slightly upward? Simply educating one's eye to visually average the peaks and valleys and determine the overall slant or pitch[5] that the graph, or portion of the graph, is taking will give you the trend of that graph or portion of that graph for that period.

Sit back and look at the following graph, which reflects six weeks' worth of stats. It will be seen that the overall slant of the graph is slightly up. The Condition by six-week trend is NORMAL.

---

[5] **pitch:** the degree of inclination or slope; angle.

CORRECT METHOD

Results in a NORMAL Trend Interpretation

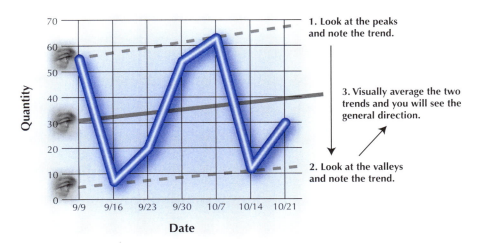

Reading stat trends by drawing a line midpoint between the first and last graph lines does not always result in an incorrect Condition assignment; one would assign the correct Condition about fifty percent of the time. That is not good enough and the system should not be used. If you have ever relied on such a system of drawing lines on the graph to come up with a trend, eliminate that false datum and reeducate your eye to simply spot the pitch or slant of the overall direction of the stat by LOOKING.

The following example, using the same six weeks of stats, shows how one would arrive at a false conclusion, an *incorrect Condition by trend*, by using the faulty system of drawing a line midpoint between the first and last graph lines.

INCORRECT METHOD

Results in an EMERGENCY Trend Interpretation

The arrow indicates the statistic is Emergency trending. This is INCORRECT and an INCORRECT METHOD of determining a trend.

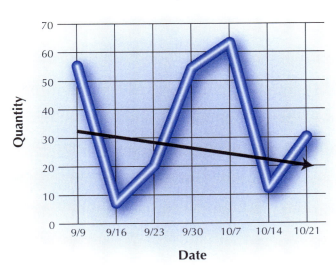

The following examples show various statistic trends and the Conditions that would be assigned (providing that the graphs are properly scaled).

A Non-Existence *trend* would look like this:

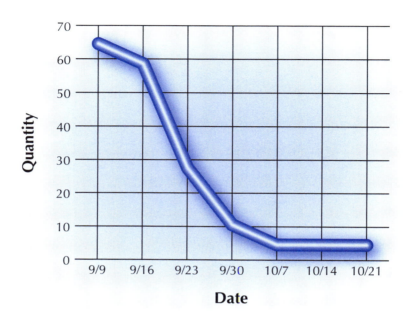

This would also be a Non-Existence *trend*:

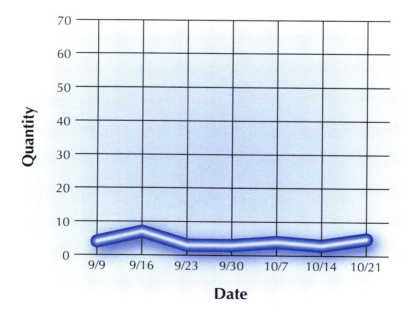

This would be a Danger *trend*:

This would be an Emergency *trend*:

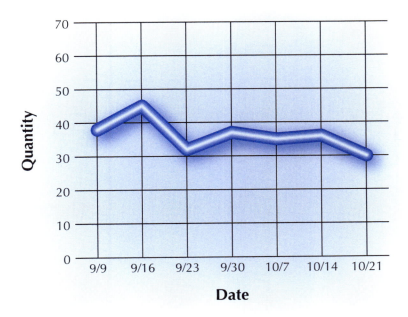

As one can see, it is not as steep a decline as a Danger trend.

This would also be an Emergency *trend* as it *will* collapse — nothing stays level for long.

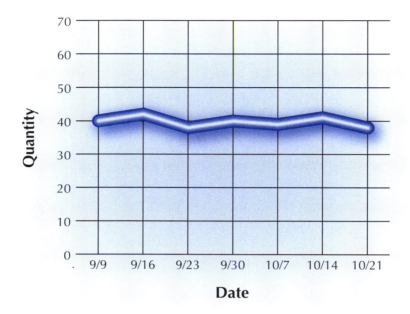

This would be a Normal *trend*:

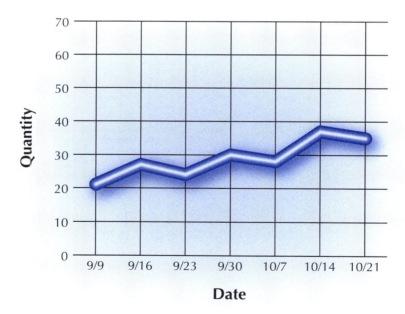

Any slight rise above level is Normal.

This would be an Affluence *trend*:

Power is a Normal trend maintained in a high, high range.

This would be a Power *trend*:

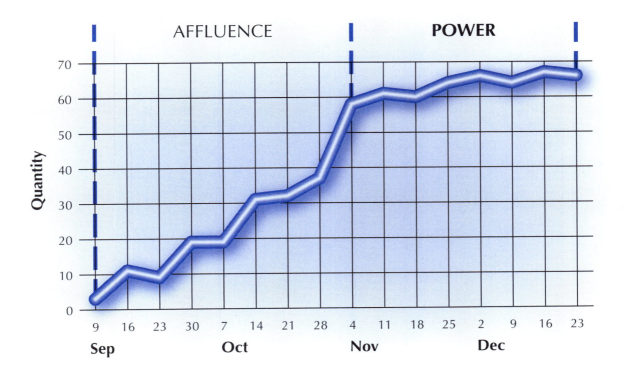

PROPERLY SCALING STATISTIC GRAPHS

Correct scaling is vital to reading a graph.

As previously noted, a *graph* is a line or diagram showing how one quantity depends on, compares with or changes another. It is any pictorial device used to display numerical relationships.

A graph is not informative if its vertical scale results in graph line changes that are too small. It is not possible to draw the graph at all if the line changes are too large.

If the ups and downs are not plainly visible on a graph, then those interpreting the graph make errors. What is shown as a flat-looking line really should be a mountain range.

VERTICAL SCALE

By SCALE is meant the number of anything per vertical inch of graph. Scale is different for every statistic.

The way to do a scale is as follows:

1. Determine the lowest amount one expects a particular statistic to go — this is not always zero.

2. Determine the highest amount one can believe the statistic will go in the next three months.

3. Subtract (1) from (2).

4. Proportion the vertical divisions as per (3).

Your scale will then be quite real and show up its rises and falls.

The element of hope can enter too strongly into a graph. That is, one might be inclined to scale a graph with a vertical range that exceeds his current level of production by 500%, for example, with the hope that he will attain that level in a year. One shouldn't scale a graph that covers the next few months with a numerical range that is unlikely to be reached in that time frame. Furthermore, one need not figure a scale for more than one graph at a time. If you go onto a new piece of graph paper, figure the scale all out again; and as the organization rises in activity, sheet by sheet the scale can be accommodated.

HORIZONTAL SCALE

On horizontal time scale, try not to exceed 3 months, as one can get that scale too condensed too. Conversely, if too little time is plotted, the scale can become too spread out where again it looks like a flat line and, thus, it misinforms.

Here is an *incorrect* example: We take an organization that runs at $5,000 per week. We proportion the vertical marks of the graph paper of which there are 10, so each one represents $10,000. When graphed, this will show a low line, quite flat, no matter what the organization income is doing and so draws no attention from executives when it rises and dives.

INCORRECTLY SCALED GRAPH

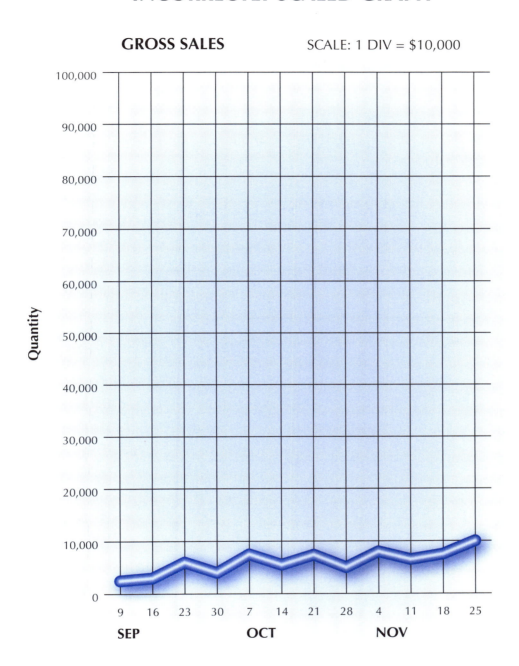

This is the *correct* way to do it for gross income for a company averaging $5,000 per week:

1. Looking over the old graphs of the past 6 months we find it never went under $2,400. So we take $2,000 as the lowest point of the graph paper.

2. We estimate this company should get up to $12,000 on occasion in the next 3 months, so we take this as the top of the graph paper.

3. We subtract $2,000 from $12,000 and we have $10,000.

4. We take the 10 blocks of vertical and make each one $1,000, starting with $2,000 as the lowest mark.

Now we plot gross income as $1,000 per graph division.

This will look right, show falls and rises very clearly and so will be of use to executives in interpretation. [See sample graph below.]

Try to use easily computed units like 5, 10, 25, 50 or 100, and show the scale itself on the graph; e.g., 1 DIV = 100.

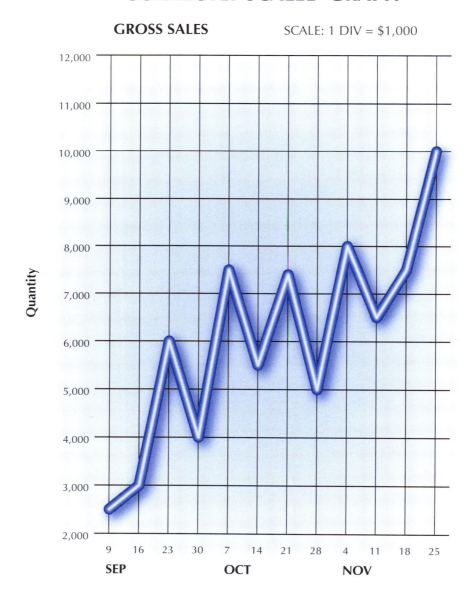

Correct scaling is the essence of good graphing.

Chapter 14

TARGETING OF STATISTICS AND QUOTAS

As stated previously, a statistic is a number or amount *compared* to an earlier number or amount of the same thing. *Statistics* refer to the quantity of work done or the value of it in money.

In an organization, every division, every department and every job should have an assigned statistic which represents its work or production. Also in any organization there should always be some individual assigned as responsible for the work or production of every division, every department and every job position. Examples:

Job	Person Responsible	Statistic
Receptionist	Ellen	Particles Routed (#)
Director of Personnel	Lisa	Persons Hired & Started (#)
Telemarketer	Craig	Sales Made (#)
Sales Manager	Margaret	Units Sold (#)
Director of Income	Ginny	Money Collected ($)
Director of Disbursements	Jack	Bills Paid ($)
VP of Delivery Division	Sue	Programs Delivered (#)

An employee should be required to report weekly the statistic of every job position for which he or she is responsible. To do this, the employee would have to keep a daily running record of such statistics. In this way, it is possible to (1) compare the statistic of one day to the statistic of the day before, (2) to predict by computation the projected statistic for the week as compared to the already reported statistic of the past week and (3) to cause actions to occur which lead to the increase of the daily statistic and to the ultimate increase of the weekly statistic.

QUOTAS

Quota is defined as a production assignment. It would be the number assigned to whatever is produced. For instance, a telemarketer is given the quota of 10 sales to make per day or 50 sales per week.

Quotas *can* be set for subproducts and *should* be.

Example: Previously, we created a subproducts list for a seminar coordinator's VFP. From that BE-DO-HAVE list, we must work out the subproducts of the VFP that one can actually quota. For instance, we could not quota "someone hatted to coordinate seminars", "schedule flights", "mail welcome packets" or "time to schedule seminar." It is necessary to determine the measurable subproducts for which quotas can be set and which, when accomplished, add up to a VFP.

> **SEMINAR COORDINATOR**
>
> **VFP:** Well planned and successfully delivered seminars.
>
> **MEASURABLE SUBPRODUCTS**
>
> 1. Scheduled seminars (e.g., quota: 6 per year)
> 2. Confirmed attendees (e.g., quota: 225 for seminar #1)
> 3. Completed staff itineraries (e.g., quota: 6 for seminar #1)
> 4. Completed conference room setup checklist (e.g., quota: complete 28 of 28 items)
> 5. Attendees present at seminar (e.g., quota: 200 for seminar #1)

Setting quotas does result in subproducts which result in VFPs, and should be done.

TARGETING

TARGET is defined as an objective one intends to accomplish within a given period of time.

TARGETING is defined as establishing what action or actions should be undertaken in order to achieve a desired objective.

In the case of Craig, the telemarketer, who is given the quota of "10 sales per day", it would be as simple as obtaining from the sales manager the necessary leads, making 50 phone calls, conducting 25 interviews, closing 10 prospects and determining to remain on the job until this was accomplished.

Any quota can be targeted for increase daily and weekly. For instance, Craig can set a target of 2 extra sales per day over that of the day before. This would mean he would make 12 sales one day, 14 sales the next day, 16 sales the day after that, and so on. If he were to achieve his targeted increase each day, he will have made 80 sales by the end of the week. That is a 60% increase over the original quota of 50 sales per week!

In highly successful organizations, the practice of setting quotas and targeting has been in use for some time.

The senior-most executive of the organization (e.g., owner, CEO, executive director) or his designated representative (e.g., office manager) establishes with the division heads (1) exactly what quotas will be for the weekly divisional statistics in order to increase them over those of the previous week and (2) HOW this will be done. The division heads should do the same with their department directors, the directors with their section in-charges, and the section in-charges with the personnel under them.

The quotas established must be real and always higher than those of the week before, with the idea in mind of creating a continually rising statistical graph. If this is done, the statistics rise, the organization expands, and more personnel are hired, apprenticed and trained on their job positions so that more production can occur to keep the statistics rising.

The targeting of actions necessary to accomplish the quotas must be definite, conform to company policy, and be *doable*. Do not permit nebulous generalities to occur on the targeting cycle of action, as nothing will be accomplished and no quotas achieved.

Additionally, when you determine the Condition of your statistic for the week and write your Condition formula, you should include in that write-up the specific targeting actions that you determined will achieve your quota. By doing so, you will make the steps of the formula more specific and in accordance with the goals you set for yourself.

Let's take the example of the telemarketer above. His statistic for the week is in Danger.

His supervisor gives him a quota of 10 sales per day, 50 sales for the week. If achieved, Craig's stats will be nicely up over the week before. However, Craig wishes to completely revert his statistic and achieve 80 sales for the week.

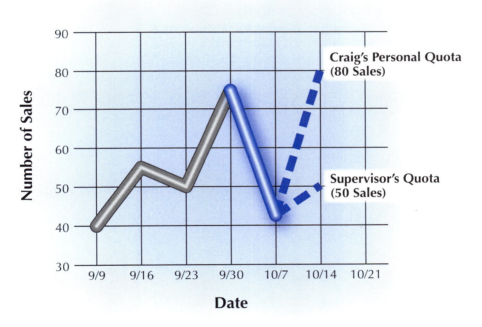

He sets for himself a target of 2 extra sales per day over that of the day before. To accomplish this, Craig determines that he'll have to obtain from the sales manager 300 leads, make 250 phone calls and conduct 150 interviews in order to close 80 prospects.

Here's what Craig's Danger Condition formula might look like:

DANGER FORMULA

1. **Bypass habits or normal routines.**

    One of my habits has been to take an extended break after just 3 phone calls. Consequently, I lose momentum and find it difficult to immediately get back in the groove. I will only take a break once per hour, so that I can make at least 50 phone calls per day.

It has been a normal routine for me to call a lead just once. If I get a busy signal or no answer, I put the lead in an "inactive" file folder. This wastes what potentially could be a new client. I'm going to keep all leads active this week until I reach them.

I've been arriving at work at least 15 minutes late every morning due to traffic congestion. I will get up earlier and leave the house at least 20 minutes sooner than I have been.

2. **Handle the situation and any danger in it.**

   My sales dropped to just 40 last week. I am producing well below my average for the past year of 60 sales per week. I need to revert my statistic. To do this, I will obtain 300 leads from the sales manager, make 50 phone calls per day and conduct 30 interviews per day. That should result in 80 sales for the week.

3. **Assign self a Danger Condition.**

   I am in a Danger Condition.

4. **Get in your own personal ethics by finding what you are doing that is out-ethics and use self-discipline to correct it and get honest and straight.**

   I have been goofing off too much during the workday. I have only been on the phone talking to prospects an average of 5 hours a day. I've been spending the remaining time on the phone doing personal business or surfing the Internet. From now on, I will not conduct any routine personal business while on the job. I will only use the Internet during authorized breaks.

   I will remain on the job until my targets are accomplished.

5. **Reorganize your life so that the dangerous situation is not continually happening to you.**

   I will monitor my production on an hourly basis to ensure that I meet my daily quota. At the end of each day, I will evaluate my production so far for the week and make the appropriate adjustments to my targeting actions, so that I'll achieve my quota by the end of the week.

   I will make sure I get my personal business, like paying bills online, done at home well before posted deadlines, so that I don't have to do it at work just to avoid late charges.

6. **Formulate and adopt firm policy that will hereafter detect and prevent the same situation from continuing to occur.**

   Whenever I'm not meeting my daily quota, I won't wait until the week is almost over to get with the sales manager and I won't wait until the sales manager comes to me. I will go to him for help as soon as I realize I'm having trouble.

   If I feel that I have a scarcity of leads, I will first check to see that I haven't wasted any. I will never discard a lead because I had difficulty contacting the person. I will always call on a lead at least once a day, for up to two weeks, until I reach him. At the end of that period of time, I will return the lead to the sales manager if I have been unsuccessful in making contact.

DAILY GRAPHS

Each employee who can measure his production (products and subproducts) on a daily basis must keep a **daily graph** of his statistic and an **accumulating graph** for the week, both on the same graph sheet. An accumulating graph merely means you keep adding one day's statistic to those of the day before.

Additionally, one could monitor his *daily* progress in reaching the quota set for the week by drawing a line on the same graph, from zero at the beginning of the week, to the amount of the targeted quota at the end of the week. When drawn this way, the **quota line** breaks down the weekly quota into equal daily quotas. If the accumulating graph line reaches or exceeds the quota line each day, that would assure one of achieving his quota by the end of the week.

Example: Bob is a salesman whose VFP is gross income. His manager has set his production quota at $9,000 for the coming week. Bob created a graph with a quota line set from zero to $9,000. Bob would have to produce $1,800 in income each day in order to make his quota. The graph below shows the quota line, as well as the daily graph and the accumulating graph for the week's statistics.

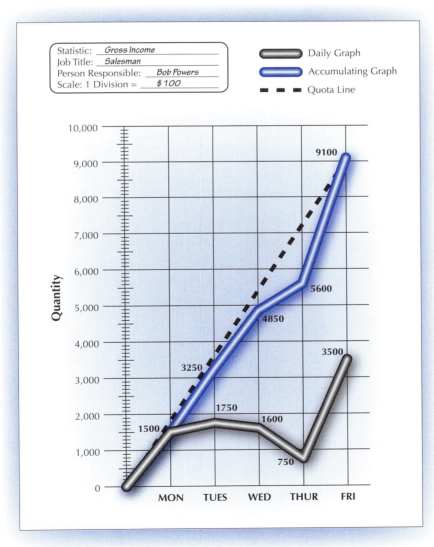

Managers and supervisors check these graphs daily with their juniors. From these graphs it is easy to see whether the statistics are rising, whether quotas are being met and whether the statistics will be higher than those of the prior week.

By monitoring daily graphs:

1. **Targets can be unbugged.**[1]

    Referring to the previous illustrated example, the sales manager gave Bob a weekly quota of $9,000 in personal production. His daily quota was $1,800. By the end of the day on Thursday, his accumulated income was only $5,600, $1,600 less than the $7,200 quota for four days of production. Furthermore, Bob had made only $750 in sales on Thursday. Upon checking his daily graph, Bob's supervisor, Josie, observed that his total sales to date were well below the quota line. She further noted that his target of conducting 30 interviews per day had stalled. He had only conducted 84 interviews during a 4-day period for which he targeted doing 120. Josie asked Bob if he had run into any difficulties during the past few days. Bob recalled that a customer was very rude and insulting to him on Tuesday and from that point on, he just wasn't doing as well on the job. Josie got him to see that the customer intended to upset him and that it resulted in his unwillingness to reach out to new customers. Bob brightened up and felt re-energized to meet his quota.

    New targets can be established.

    Continuing with the example above, Josie worked out with Bob HOW he could reach $9,000 in sales by the end of the week. She set a quota of $3,400 for the day. To achieve that quota, he targeted himself to make 75 phone calls, conduct 45 interviews and close 17 deals averaging $200 each. He worked hard the rest of the day and achieved his highest daily statistic in weeks – $3,500. Bob surpassed his quota, making $9,100 for the week.

    New quotas can be projected.

    In the event that one makes his quota prior to the end of the week, his senior would project a new quota. For example, if a sales manager gave his junior the quota of $10,000 for the week and he reached it by the end of the day on Wednesday, the manager would project a new quota for the week. As stated previously, the quota established must be real.

2. or **Hatting and more establishing can occur.**

    Continuing with the example above, Josie realized that Bob was not hatted to handle rude and insulting customers. She sent him to the staff trainer to learn the company's established protocol for handling belligerent customers. Josie also checked to ensure that her other sales reps were hatted in this protocol as well.

3. or **Ethics can be put in where the individual appears incapable of keeping his own in.**

    Let's say that Bob had already experienced a rude customer in the past and Josie helped him get unbugged. She trained him on the proper handling of such customers. Then he ran into the same situation a few more times and, each time, he got into an argument

---

[1] **unbugged:** (*slang*) unsnarled or gotten moving again.

with the customer. This caused public relations problems that had to be addressed by the owner of the company. Bob's production went down afterwards in every instance. Despite verbal warnings, he did not take responsibility to get better trained and to apply what he had learned. In this scenario, Bob demonstrated that he is incapable of keeping his ethics in, where handling belligerent customers is concerned. Josie proceeded to put his ethics in by writing a report on him and telling him that the matter would be addressed in his annual performance evaluation. Bob got the message and immediately took responsibility for the situation. He practiced how to handle difficult customers and he worked late to get his statistics up. He made his quota by the end of the week.

A set time can be determined *daily* as to when each employee should have his graph posted for inspection. Seniors can then easily make their inspections without being delayed while someone computes and posts his graph.

By setting quotas and establishing targets that will achieve the quotas, an executive can get his statistics rising.

Planning

Chapter 15

BATTLE PLANS

Battle plan is defined as a written list of doable targets to be executed in the immediate short-term future (i.e., the coming day or week) that will implement and accomplish some portion of a strategic plan.

Strategy is a plan for the skillful overall conduct of a large field of operations, or a sector of such operations, toward the achievement of a specific goal or result. This is planning that is done at upper-echelon[1] level, as, if it is to be effective, it must be done from an overview of the broad existing situation. It is the central strategy worked out at the top which, like an umbrella, covers the activities of the echelons below it.

Some people write "battle plans" as just a series of actions which they hope to get done in the coming day or week. This is fine and better than nothing and does give some orientation to one's actions. In fact someone who does not do this is quite likely to get far less done and be considerably more harassed and "busy" than one who does. An orderly planning of what one intends to do in the coming day or week and then getting it done is an excellent way to achieve production. But this is using "battle planning" in an irreducible-minimum form as a tool.

Why is this called a "battle plan" in the first place? It seems a very harsh military term to apply to the workaday world of admin. But it is a very appropriate term.

A war is something that happens over a long period of time. The fate of everything depends on it. A battle is something that occurs in a short unit of time. One can lose several battles and still win a war. Thus one, in essence, is talking about short periods of time when one is talking about a battle plan.

In military terms, strategic planning would concern the overall conduct of a war or a sector of it. Below strategic planning one has tactical planning. There is a very, very great difference between a strategic plan and a tactical plan. While tactical planning is used to win an engagement,[2] strategic planning is used to win the full campaign.[3] While the strategic plan is the large-scale, long-range plan to ensure victory, a tactical plan tells exactly who to move what to where and exactly what to do at that point. The tactical plan must integrate into the strategic plan and accomplish the strategic plan. And it must do this with precise, doable targets. And that, in essence, is management.

---

[1] **upper echelon:** the higher level of any group. In business organizations, this refers to senior executives. [Example: *Mark's new customer service campaign involved employees at every level, including the **upper echelon**.*]

[2] **engagement:** a hostile encounter; a battle.

[3] **campaign:** a series of military operations undertaken to achieve a large-scale objective during a war. [Example: *Grant's Vicksburg **campaign** secured the entire Mississippi for the Union.*]

Like the military, management of a company is at its best when there is a strategic plan and when it is known at least down to the level of tactical planners, i.e., "middle management" — the heads of departments and divisions. And tactical planners are simply those people putting strategic plans into programs[4] and projects[5] that are written in doable target form, which are then known to and executed from middle management on down. The person doing the target might not be aware of the overall strategic plan or how his target fits into it, but it is a very poor management indeed whose targets do not *all* implement to one degree or another the overall strategic plan.

This is how it is supposed to work: The upper planning body (senior executives) turns out a strategic plan. Middle management (division and department heads) turn this strategic plan into tactical orders. They do this on a long-term basis (tactical plans, programs and projects) and a short-term basis. When you get on down to the short-term basis you have battle plans. When one is talking about "mini programs" in an organization, one is actually talking about small battle plans at the lowest tactical levels. These must be based upon a middle-management tactical plan and this, in turn, must be based on a strategic plan.

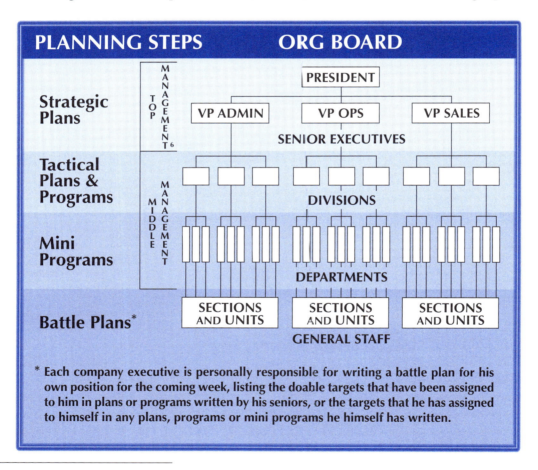

---

[4] **program:** a series of steps in sequence to carry out a plan. **Programs** are written at division level or above and are made up of all types of targets coordinated and executed on time. **Programs** written and executed at departmental level in a company are called **mini programs**.

[5] **project:** a series of guiding steps written in sequence to carry out one step of a program, which, if followed, will result in a full and successful accomplishment of the program target.

[6] **top management:** the highest ranking executives (with titles such as Chief Executive Officer, President, Vice President, Executive Director, etc.) responsible for the entire organization. **Top management** lays down and/or okays policy, programs and plans.

There is one thing to beware of in doing battle plans. One can write a great many targets which have little or nothing to do with the strategic plan and which keep people terribly busy and which accomplish no part of the overall strategic plan. Thus a battle plan can become a liability since it is not pushing any overall strategic plan and is not accomplishing any tactical objective.

The understanding and competent use of targeting in battle plans is vital to the overall accomplishment that raises production, income, delivery or anything else that is a desirable end.

NOTE: In order to ensure that you actually apply the steps of the formula for the Condition you're in, you may include in your battle plan the specific actions worked out in your weekly Condition formula. Whatever your Condition is at the end of the week, work out how you would apply the formula steps in relation to your job, and add those actions at the beginning of your battle plan. Other battle plan targets based on strategic plans and programs would also be included, but the weekly Condition handling steps could also be a part of it. In this way, all your targets for the week, both Condition targets and program targets, would be listed in just one place. This is a very convenient and efficient way to operate.

Example: Let's continue with the example of Craig, the telemarketer, whose Danger Formula was provided on pages 89-90 in the previous chapter entitled *Targeting of Statistics and Quotas*. The company wants to expand and has decided to market new services to other professions (accountants and optometrists). The Senior Vice President for Sales has written a strategic plan. The Sales Director, in turn, has written a program based on that plan, and Craig must now write his battle plan using the doable targets his boss laid out for him in the program. His battle plan for the week could look like this:

BATTLE PLAN
Week Ending: 10/14

Name: Craig Cassidy **Job Position:** Telemarketer
Condition: Danger

Weekly Condition Action Items **Done**

1. Obtain 300 leads from Sales Manager ✓
2. Make 250 phone calls, 50 per day ✓M ✓T ✓W __Th __F
3. Conduct 150 interviews, 30 per day ✓M ✓T __W __Th __F
4. Make 80 sales this week

Program Targets **Deadline** **Done**

1. Rehearse marketing survey 10/11 ✓
2. Contact and survey 15 Accountants 10/13 __
3. Contact and survey 15 Optometrists 10/13 ✓
4. Report survey results to Director of Sales 10/14 __

Chapter 16

COORDINATION

COORDINATION is the essence of management. The word "management" implies there is *something* and some *someones* to manage. A *business* or *company* or *organization* implies others are present and are engaged in a similar activity. It is a *team*.

Any organization, no matter how complex, is bound together by common purposes. If the different parts of such an organization are not *coordinated*, they begin to cross each other's lines and tangle. With such a tangle, one gets no forward progress. The employees can be numerous, appear busy, even frantic, yet no production is really accomplished.

What is missing is COORDINATION. The efforts of each part of the organization are not being directed and meshed into flows that would achieve the common purpose.

THAT is what a manager is for. The manager and his immediate assistants have to *know* where they are going and have to make certain each part of the organization knows; they also have to make certain that the efforts of each individual segment of the organization are devoted to forwarding the same general purpose.

When we speak of *coordination*, we are really talking about conceiving or overseeing a strategic plan into the tactical version and, at the lower echelon, coordinating the actions of those who will do the actual things necessary to carry it out so that they all align in one direction.

The elements of coordination are *planning, knowledge, information, agreement* and *production*. Good coordination of team effort results in high ARC. This is called "team spirit", "morale", "esprit de corps", etc. But what it is, in fact, is agreement and understanding within the team so they can each forward the general purpose of the group. Coordination is why companies have executive board meetings, conferences, staff meetings, mini programs for departments, etc. It is even why they have an org board.

WEEKLY STAFF MEETINGS

Employees should be gathered together, once a week, to hold a staff meeting. A weekly staff meeting is not just a meeting where someone in charge lectures the group. The purpose of the staff meeting is to develop a team spirit of mutual cooperation and coordination. The owner, president or executive director runs the staff meeting.

Each person is responsible for his own stat or the stats of his sector (unit, section, department, etc.) and, at the meeting, must personally report on them and show the graph or graphs.

Some of the topics routinely covered in a staff meeting are:

1. General business announcements.

2. Presentation of stats and trends by individual staff members and a Condition assigned to each stat with a battle plan for each. In a large organization where it isn't feasible for each employee to present his individual stat and battle plan, the company's senior executives would determine which stats and battle plans are to be presented. Minimally, this would include departmental and divisional stats. Stats must be real and represent actual production, leading toward a VFP.

3. The Condition of the whole group. (NOTE: The group Condition is not based on one particular statistic. It is essentially a summary of the specific statistic-based weekly Conditions assigned to the divisions of the company.)

4. Combined battle plan.

Each person in the group is personally responsible for:

➤ Having a correct stat which reflects production factually

➤ The stats of his area of responsibility

➤ Graphing the stat or stats on time

➤ Presenting the stat and any clarifications

➤ Presenting a battle plan for each stat for the coming week

➤ Full knowledge of reading stats, date coincidence,[1] stat interpretation and Conditions.

---

[1] **date coincidence:** When statistics change radically for better or for worse, look for the last major alteration or broad general action that occurred just before it and it is usually the reason for the change. In other words, a specific major change in what one normally did or does could result in a dramatically changed statistic. All one need do is ask, "What changed?" when looking at a radical increase or decrease in a statistic, and he will find the occurrence that coincided with the changed statistic and the date that it happened. We call this the **date coincidence**. Once spotted, one can then take the appropriate action to reverse the decline or reinforce the increase in the statistic.

Office Efficiency

Chapter 17

COMPANY COMMUNICATIONS SYSTEM

MEMORANDUMS

A memorandum, or *memo*, is a communication, usually brief, written for interoffice circulation. It may contain directive, advisory or informative matter.

There are two basic types of memos: those that require a response and those that don't. Memos that require responses are sometimes called dispatches.

An interoffice memo is a simple thing. You can keep a copy if you want, but only one copy (the original) goes and comes back.

When writing a memo, address it to the *JOB POSITION*—NOT the person. (If a person changes job positions, or leaves, if you address the memo to the *position*, it will be received by the new occupant of the position; but if you address it to the *person*, it may not be received and handled if the person leaves.)

Set up a memo as follows:

➢ For information or advice:

MEMORANDUM

To: Sales Manager
From: Marketing Director   Date: Sep 23

Dear Bob,

Please take a look at the attached brochure. I would like your comments regarding the price list and product descriptions. Please respond no later than 5 p.m. today. We're going to the printer in the morning.

Regards,
Teri

➢ For a request or an order:

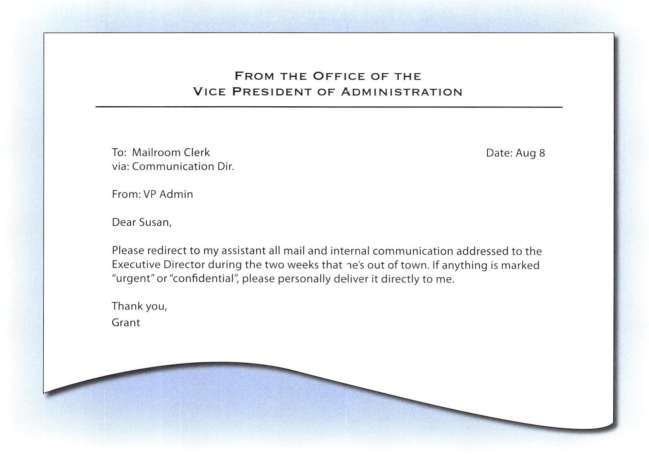

This format is used so that when it is ready to be returned, an arrow can be drawn pointing to the position to which it is to be returned, eliminating the need to write it. If the message is one that should go in your hat, either put it in your hat and acknowledge sender, or photocopy it for your hat, returning the original to sender. If a memo regarding anything done or to be done below your level comes to you from a junior, always insist he has attested it is "okay". If you, in turn, wish to send it on, you too must attest it is "okay" and send it on. If it is "not okay", return the memo to the originator stating briefly why it is not okay. Always require the junior to state or initial "This is okay" on all work, actions or projects.

The receiver handles the memo and *retains* the memo until such time as it has been completely handled. If it is a matter which involves days or weeks, you can send a separate memo to the sender stating, for example, "_____ *is being attended to. You may expect it to be completed within five days.*"—but retain the original memo until the job is done, *then* return it to sender marked "DONE". Do not return the original with "It's being attended to." Originals only return with "DONE" or "Can't be done." Otherwise the communication stays incomplete. When replying to a memo, put down the date of the message.

Hardcopy memos can be handwritten rather than typed. Memos can also be sent electronically via e-mail. If your company is equipped with a computer network and authorizes its use for internal communications, memos that do not require a response may be sent. However, the receiver should print e-mailed memos that do require a response. As stated above, the receiver *retains* the memo until such time as it has been completely handled. It is important to a company that memos requiring action are visible and accessible to others in the event of an employee's absence. Have you ever tried to find a document among hundreds of saved e-mail files in a fellow employee's e-mail in-box when he's out sick? It's virtually impossible. And if you don't know his password, you won't have access at all! So it's best to keep interoffice communication requiring action and response out in the open and on the traditional communication lines of the company.

PUTTING REQUESTS IN WRITING

If you have a request, put it in writing. Do not go to the person and expect him to carry your request around in his head. Personnel are not supposed to present their bodies, or their bodies with a memo, to other personnel except for actual conferences, which are kept to a minimum. Few things need conferences. Memos take care of 99 percent of organizational business.

RESPONDING TO COMMUNICATIONS

Handle your memos daily. Do not let them stack up on you. When someone sends you a memo let him hear from you. Do not get the reputation of "I hesitate to send so-and-so a memo because I don't know when I'll hear from him regarding it, or *if* I'll ever hear from him regarding it." DO NOT LET YOUR MEMOS DEAD-END. When you let your memos (or letters) stack up on your desk, you are in actuality chopping the communication lines of the organization.

ANSWERING LETTERS

In answering letters, answer the letter writers' questions. Give them the information they are seeking. DO NOT FAIL TO ANSWER THEIR QUESTIONS. If you don't know the answers, find out.

THE COMM CENTER & COMM STATIONS

The Comm Center, or Communication Center, is usually located in the Human Resources or main administrative department in a company. The Comm Center contains a basket for each employee. Each basket is tagged with the person's name and underneath the name is his or her job title(s). Each person is responsible for delivering his own memos to the proper baskets and for picking up his own memos daily. Do not fail to pick up your memos at least twice a day (once in the morning and once in the afternoon — make your own schedule). But do not let memos pile up in your basket.

In larger organizations, a Comm Center and separate divisional comm centers may be instituted. The Comm Center would consist of one basket for each division. Each divisional comm center is placed in the divisional working area with a basket for each employee in that division plus a divisional in-basket and a divisional out-basket. The Communications Department manager would be responsible for delivering memos into the divisional in-baskets and from the divisional out-baskets into the Comm Center baskets. The division manager's secretary is responsible for the distribution of memos from the divisional in-basket to employees' baskets.

Keep abreast of all job position changes. As the org board is changed, the Comm Center baskets are changed. Always know who is occupying what job position so that when you deliver a memo you will always know whose basket it goes in. If you are not sure, check the org board.

The Director of Communications sees that every employee has a basket in the Comm Center *and* a personal comm station (stack of three baskets) near his area of work *no matter who* the employee is — that includes the janitor!

The top basket, labeled "**IN**", should contain those items still to be looked at.

The middle basket, labeled "**PENDING**", is to contain those items which have been looked at but cannot be dealt with immediately.

The bottom basket, labeled "**OUT**", is to contain those items which have been dealt with and are now ready for distribution into the communication lines again, or to file, etc.

No work that is active may be put in desk drawers or hidden off the lines. All active memos must be delivered where they are going and must thereafter be visibly in stations or beanstalks[1] under visible headings.

---

[1] **beanstalk: Beanstalk** is a trade name of Beanstalk Shelving Limited. **Beanstalks** are wire baskets used in communication systems in organizations. They may be attached one on top of another resulting in a system of baskets that look like a **beanstalk**.

All *in*-baskets must be kept empty. When an *in* is viewed but not done, it goes into the person's *pending*.

It *must* be possible to locate any active memo on the lines whether it is a business day or not.

Keep your basket station straight. Keep your *in*-basket empty. And keep current work visible and where it belongs on the lines.

One can always judge the state of a department by the state of its comm stations.

Chapter 18

COMPLETED STAFF WORK
How to Get Approval of Actions and Projects

THE MOST IMPORTANT PIECE OF YOUR HAT

The term *"Completed Staff Work"* means—an assembled package of information on any given situation, plan or emergency, forwarded to a senior sufficiently complete to require from that senior only an "Approved" or "Disapproved". Completed Staff Works (CSWs) are employed in order to reduce dev-t[1] and increase speed of action.

Here is what slows down approval and action and develops traffic:

Somebody sends his senior a skimpy piece of information and demands a solution. As more information is required than is presented, the senior must then take over the person's hat and assemble the missing data using his own time and lines. He must then dream up a solution and then order an action to be taken. This causes a slowdown on any action, causes his lines, already loaded, to be used for information assembly and brings about a feeling of emergency. His *pending* basket overloads and confusion results. This would be called "Incomplete Staff Work". It is incomplete because the senior has to complete it by:

1. Assembling the data necessary for a solution

2. Dreaming up the solution based on written data only

3. Issuing orders (he must write himself) rather than approving orders (proposed by his junior).

If you are mad at your boss, you can always ruin him with "Incomplete Staff Work". You forward him a fragment of alarming data without collecting the whole picture. This makes him do a full job of information collection. You give him no recommended solution. This makes him have to achieve[2] a solution by remote examination of data; such solutions are often wrong as they are made without full data. Then you make him issue arbitrary and forceful orders that may ARC break some area and hurt his reputation. That's how to get even with a boss. And even if there's no intention of harming him, sending "Incomplete Staff Work" to your boss *does* harm him by making him send for information—getting memos on already crowded lines, by making him guess at the situation, by making him cook up solutions which may be unreal, and by thrusting him into the role of an arbitrary tyrant.

---

[1] **dev-t:** [**dev**eloped **t**raffic] unusual and unnecessary traffic.

[2] **achieve:** to get or attain by effort; obtain. [Examples: *to **achieve** a solution, to **achieve** victory*]

Now that we've seen the negative side, let us examine the positive side.

"Completed Staff Work" is an assembled memo or packet that:

1. States the situation

2. Gives all the data necessary to its solution

3. Advises a solution

4. Contains a line for approval or disapproval by the senior with his signature.

If documents or letters are to be signed as part of the executive's action, they should be part of the package, all ready to sign. A *"SIGN HERE"* message tag or some similar label should indicate each place that a signature is required.

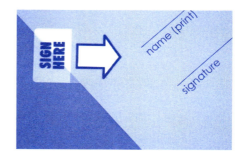

Wrong example: A memo to corporate headquarters stating:

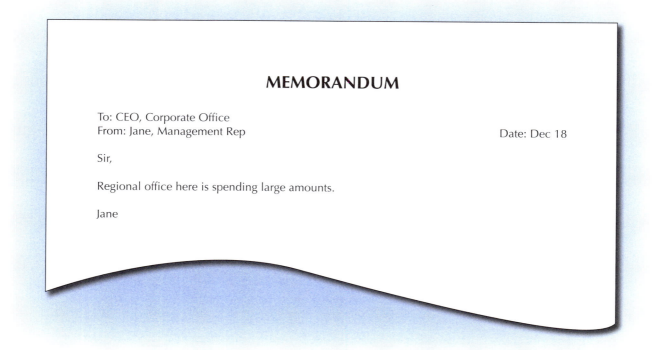

Look what the executive now has to do. He has to find out what is meant by "large amounts", who is doing it, if it is dangerous, figure out a way to curtail it and issue orders about it. *None* of this is his hat. He is being forced to wear the hat of the informing person.

Right example: The executive receives a packet with a memo on top that states:

> **MEMORANDUM**
>
> To: CEO, Corporate Office
> From: Jane Kelly, Southwest Regional Office   Date: Dec 18
>
> Dear Mr. Wagner,
>
> Regional office here is fast approaching insolvency. Data enclosed. I recommend:
>
> 1. Purchasing Agent be transferred to the position of Mailroom Clerk that is now empty and that Vince Alexander be hired to fill the Purchasing Agent position at $3,500.00 per month.
>
> 2. That the Chief Executive Officer be reprimanded for bad financial management and be ordered to budget his outgo.
>
> 3. That a purchase order system be enforced.
>
> 4. That the Director of Promotion and Marketing receive on-the-job training.
>
> This is okay.
>
> Jane Kelly
> Management Rep
>
> Approved _____   Disapproved _____

Attached are copies of financial reports showing insolvency, a summary of amounts spent in the last two months, a summary of income for the last two months and a list of trivial items bought lately at high cost.

What the executive does then is check the approval line and sign. A response is sent by his secretary: "Proposal OK. Regards, (executive's name)". The whole packet is sent back.

On receipt of the packet, the Management Representative issues the local directives and takes the other needed actions.

Action could occur because the data, solution and orders were all assembled as "Completed Staff Work".

If you want to hold down your job or remain in charge of your project, don't insist on your senior collecting the data you should collect or dreaming up the solution that you, more familiar with the scene, should achieve. And don't put him in a position of issuing unreal orders you can't then carry out.

"Completed Staff Work" is what executives want. It is the most important piece of your hat. By writing CSWs, you increase office efficiency.

If an executive returns an item you've sent him with the letters *CSWP* on it, it means "Complete the Staff Work, Please."

SAMPLE CSW FORMAT

To: *Recipient's Title*   **Date:**
From: *Sender's Title*

CSW

SITUATION: State the situation that must be resolved.

DATA: Give all the data necessary to its solution.

Attach any documents or letters needing signing.

Attach any necessary supportive data.

SOLUTION: Write out your proposed solution.

This is okay.

_____
Signature

_____
Title

Approved: _____
Disapproved: _____

Unless one can fix responsibility for actions, there is no responsibility anywhere and the organization deteriorates.

Never let a junior say "Is this okay?"

As stated previously, always require the junior to state or initial "This is okay" on all work, actions or projects.

Chapter 19

DEVELOPED TRAFFIC
The Delirium Tremens[1] of Organizations

Developed traffic is a phenomenon which costs an organization two-thirds of the effort of its employees and executives. It is condemnatory. The symbol *dev-t* means on a memo, "This memo exists only because its originator has not handled a situation, problem or an executive order." It also means "Responsibility for your job is very low." Also it means "You should be handling this without further traffic." It also means "You are manufacturing new traffic because you aren't handling old traffic."

Every time traffic is developed, somebody has flubbed. *"Developed"* traffic does *not* mean usual and necessary traffic. It means *unusual and unnecessary* traffic.

Example: Purchasing Agent is told "Buy some chairs for the courseroom." If this goes properly, the chairs simply get bought, the Purchasing Agent having estimated students, available funds and economical available materiel and arranging delivery. Purchasing Agent may have to ask a couple verbal questions of other departments to execute, but this is routine and necessary.

This can be used to develop traffic in this fashion: The executive issuing the order "Buy some chairs" is asked "How many?" "What style?" "How much?" "From what firm?" Or somebody else is asked these at length. Purchasing Department is now *worse* than a camouflaged hole.[2] Purchasing Department is making the acquisition of chairs *costly* in terms of consuming time writing memos, consuming other employees' time, upset and delay. This is dev-t.

Dev-t costs a company the services of two-thirds of its personnel. Hence, large staff, no effectiveness. An unwilling employee always makes dev-t out of every situation, problem, order and policy. Take unwilling personnel off the lines and traffic busyness drops by two-thirds and effectiveness increases by many times.

THE 51 TYPES OF DEV-T

The following is a list of items which *Dev*elop (increase) *T*raffic. It is based on years of experience with the subject of dev-t.

---

[1] **delirium tremens:** (*Latin*) also called **the d.t.'s**, a withdrawal syndrome occurring in persons who have developed physiological dependence on alcohol. It is characterized by trembling, sweating, acute anxiety, confusion and hallucinations.

[2] **camouflaged hole: Camouflage** means "disguised" or made to appear as something else. When a hat is not worn for any reason at all in an organization, one gets a breakdown, a **camouflaged hole**, at that point. Somebody has a title but doesn't do the duties or actions that go with it. It looks like there is something there, but it is actually a **hole**.

1. FALSE REPORTS

Action: Submitting a report that is false.

Result: It can cause greatly increased useless action including, at times, investigations, memos verifying it, etc.

Example: Jan works for a consulting firm. One of her duties is to confirm the attendees for the quarterly workshops held in various hotels throughout the country. She is currently confirming 280 potential attendees for the workshop to be held in Baltimore in six weeks. Jan will be taking a long-overdue vacation beginning tomorrow. More than a month ago, Diane, her supervisor, issued an order to her that she must confirm at least 200 attendees prior to leaving. As of today, she has confirmed only 128 clients. Jan knows she can't possibly confirm 72 clients in one day and she doesn't want to postpone her vacation for even a week. So she reported to Diane that she confirmed 205 clients for the workshop. Since she felt certain she would be able to reach her quota shortly after her return from vacation, she figured there was no harm in inflating her statistic. What she didn't know is that her supervisor had committed to a minimum of 200 attendees with the hotel to receive a deep discount in the cost of the guest rooms and conference room. Upon her return, Jan found it exceedingly difficult to confirm the additional 77 clients that she had already reported as confirmed. Many had already committed to attend a professional conference that had been scheduled recently for the same weekend. Jan had to tell Diane that she did not make her quota as she had reported. Diane was incensed. She felt she could no longer trust any of the statistics that Jan reported and so she ordered an investigation of Jan's area of responsibility. Further, Diane had to contact the hotel manager to negotiate a new contract, which ultimately cost the company thousands of dollars more than was budgeted. She ordered Jan to contact all the clients who were already booked for the workshop to let them know that the cost of the rooms had increased. Much of the preparatory actions done for this workshop were rendered useless, as they had to be redone. Jan was severely reprimanded for false-reporting her statistic.

2. NON COMPLIANCES

Action: Failure to comply with an order.

Result: It can set an emergency flap[3] going which crowds the lines with memos.

Example: The Human Resources Director of a large company sent an order to the facilities manager to renew the lease for the company's copy machine. He did not comply with the order. A few weeks later, without notice, the leasing company removed the copy machine from the premises. Fifty employees were astonished to find that there was no copier in the office. Each of them sent memos to the HR Director, wanting to know what happened to the copier and asking what he should do if he needs to make copies. The company came to a virtual standstill due to this flap and the HR Director's comm lines were inundated with memos.

---

[3] **flap:** something (as an incident or remark) that generates an uproar.

One consequence of noncompliance when repeated over a long period is to move a large number of targets into present time in a sort of frantic jam. Catastrophes can occur because of noncompliance.

Example: On February 5th, Sharon, the events coordinator at STAR, a network marketing company, ordered Tom, her assistant, to book a five-star hotel and conference center for the company's annual convention in May. One week later, she checked with him and he hadn't complied with her order. She told him that he would have to make arrangements by the end of the month in order for the company to meet all its other deadlines. Sharon went on emergency leave a week later and didn't return until mid-March. The first thing she did was to ask Tom what hotel he booked for the convention. Tom told her he forgot to do it. She immediately went into action to find a hotel for the convention. It took her another week to find a convention hall big enough to accommodate the event. Unfortunately, the only available dates were April 24-26. That left only four weeks to pull off the convention. Targets such as booking flights, inviting associates and reserving hotel rooms for them, printing and mailing the agendas, scheduling speakers and booking the caterer were all frantically jammed into present time to handle. None of the speakers Sharon had initially booked were available in April and 60% of the associates could not attend due to receiving such short notice. STAR suffered tremendous losses in revenue and reputation from this catastrophe.

3. ALTERED COMPLIANCE

Action: **Something was introduced or changed in the orders which made them non-optimum.**

Result: **This sometimes wastes and repeats all earlier traffic.**

Example: Rob instructed his assistant, Amy, to order new business cards for him. He told her to make sure that the cards reflect the new office address and his new job title. Amy called the printer and told him to print another order of business cards for Rob. She directed him to change Rob's job title, but she forgot to tell him to change the address. She also took it upon herself to authorize added information — Rob's cell phone number. When the cards arrived a week later, Rob was very dissatisfied, as the address had not been updated and his cell phone number, which he doesn't use for business, was printed on the cards. Amy wasted time and money. She had to reorder the cards, this time in precise compliance with Rob's order. In the meantime, Rob had to deal with a non-optimum situation — using his old business cards and making handwritten changes on them.

4. NO REPORTS

Action: **No reports.**

Result: **The scramble to find out if something has been done increases traffic. This includes lack of data forwarded as it should have been. It causes anxiety and uncertainty, as well.**

Example: Evan is responsible for shipping the training materials for the nationwide delivery of his company's workshops. Just prior to his departure on a two-week vacation to Maui, he shipped all the necessary items to the locations of each of three workshops that would be delivered in the coming week. He depleted the company's entire stock of brochures in the process. Unfortunately, Evan failed to inform anyone, prior to his departure, that he had shipped the materials. Consequently, five different people in the company, from Evan's immediate supervisor to the executive director, scrambled to find out if he had done so. No one knew how to reach him, as he didn't have a cell phone and he didn't tell anyone where he would be staying. Several people called dozens of hotels on the island. Others contacted as many of Evan's friends and family members as they could locate, to find out if they knew how to reach him. No one did. For days, the company was in a state of high anxiety, as the executives were uncertain if the materials had been sent and it was too late to have more training materials printed. Ultimately, the boxes arrived at their destinations and the trainers reported that fact. Evan was severely reprimanded when he returned from vacation. He could have avoided the whole situation by simply reporting to his senior, before he left, the data regarding the shipments.

5. COMM FORMULA[4] UNUSED

All orders out — answers in (i.e., orders sent and subsequently answered) are on the Communication Formula.

Action: **Communication Formula not used.**

Result: **Failing to answer the question asked can triple traffic.**

Example: Jerry owns a dental practice. While analyzing production statistics covering the past month, he realized that only 45% of all patients scheduled for a teeth cleaning actually showed up. So he wrote an order to Linda, the hygienist, to contact and confirm all patients who are scheduled for hygiene appointments. Also, he asked her, "How many hygiene patients are currently scheduled for the next week?" Linda responded in writing to the order, "I called all the patients." She did not answer his question. He wrote back to her, "How many hygiene patients are currently scheduled for the next week?" She replied, "I confirmed 80% so far." Jerry asked yet again, "How many hygiene patients are currently scheduled for the next week?" Finally, Linda replied, "Twenty are scheduled." Linda ultimately answered the question, but it took three memos asking the same question to get the answer. She did not use the Communication Formula, insofar as she did not give Jerry's order adequate ATTENTION and she failed to DUPLICATE and UNDERSTAND his question the first two times.

---

[4] **Communication Formula:** The Formula of Communication is: Cause, Distance, Effect with Intention, Attention and Duplication with Understanding. *CAUSE* is simply the source-point of emanation of the communication. *EFFECT* is the receipt-point of the communication. The communication goes across a *DISTANCE* from *CAUSE* to *EFFECT*. Both *CAUSE* and *EFFECT* must have *INTENTION* and give *ATTENTION*. For a true communication to take place, a *DUPLICATION* with *UNDERSTANDING* of what emanated from *CAUSE* must take place at *EFFECT*. Abbr. **Comm Formula**.

6. INFO FAILURE

Action: Those in charge fail to brief their juniors.

Result: The juniors then have no idea of what's going on and develop other traffic in conflict.

Action: Reversely, juniors fail to inform seniors of data they have.

Result: Lacking complete data, seniors could have an incorrect idea of a situation. When basing actions or orders on omitted data, one then makes a mistake.

> *Example: A company's senior executives made the decision to discontinue sales of one of their less popular products. It had not been generating sufficient profit to offset expenses associated with its manufacture or storage. However, no one bothered to inform the sales team of the change. Three sales reps subsequently sold a total of 24 units of the discontinued product. The company was placed in the dilemma of having to either (1) special order the product for the customers or (2) contact each one of them, apologize for the confusion and try to sell a substitute product.*

7. LACK OF CSW

Action: Failure to forward an assembled package of information on any given situation, plan or emergency, or failure to forward complete information on any memo, sufficiently complete to require only an "approved" or "disapproved".

Result: It slows down approval and action. It often requires returning for completed staff work, or the senior concerned must take over the person's hat and assemble the missing data using his own time and lines. And thus traffic develops.

> *Example: John, the head of the parts department of an auto body shop, sent a memo to Sam, the shop owner, informing him that a sales rep from an aftermarket[5] supply company had visited the shop earlier in the day, offering to sell them reconditioned parts at a significant discount. Giving no specifics, John wrote that the inventory was running very low on quite a few items, and he recommended that Sam act fast to replenish those items with reconditioned parts rather than new parts. Sam read the note after John had already left for the day. Due to the apparent urgency of the situation and the fact that John would not be back to work for a couple of days, Sam was forced to roll up his sleeves and spend most of the next day doing an inventory of the stockroom to determine which parts were in short supply and, of those, which ones should be replenished with reconditioned parts. To do so, he had to consult the shop foreman to ascertain which items would be appropriate to replace with reconditioned parts and he had to compare the current supplier's price list with that of the new company. Only after assembling this missing data and reviewing it could Sam make an informed decision.*

---

[5] **aftermarket:** the market for replacement parts, accessories and equipment for the care or enhancement of the original product, especially an automobile, after its sale to the consumer. [Example: *The company holds a large share in the automotive radio* **aftermarket**.]

8. SUPPRESSION ON LINES

Action: Lines get closed by arbitraries.[6]

Result: Vital info does not get through or vital action is not ordered.

Example: Sandy is the president of a graphic design company consisting of 35 employees. Long ago, she established an "open door" policy, which states that any employee may request and receive an appointment to meet with her to discuss matters of potential concern to the company or the employee's relationship to it. Sandy's assistant, Melissa, is responsible for scheduling those appointments when requested. Last week, Melissa sent out a memo to all the employees which stated that no "open door" appointments would be made without the employee first meeting with her to discuss what it is he or she would like to discuss with Sandy. Melissa had decided that Sandy's workday was being unnecessarily interrupted with matters that Melissa could address. As a consequence of that arbitrary, many of the staff were reluctant to set an appointment to meet with Sandy, and in some cases, Melissa sent the employees away, stating that the concerns or ideas they expressed to her were not of value to the company. Sandy knew nothing about Melissa's actions; consequently, she was denied vital information from her staff on matters such as their morale and bright ideas they might have to improve company production. Melissa suppressed Sandy's comm lines to her employees.

9. CROSS ORDERS

Action: Juniors issue so many orders unknown to a senior and *across* his lines.

Result: A senior's orders are obscured or lost. Things get very confused, very active, but nonproductive.

Example: The CEO issued a standing order[7] six months ago, stating that whenever a letter addressed to a client is returned to the company stamped "Address Unknown" or if it reflects a new forwarding address, the File Clerk is to update the client database with that information within 24 hours of receipt. Unbeknownst to the CEO, the VP of Administration issued an order to the receptionist to place all mail returned by the post office as "undeliverable" into a folder marked "Central Files Update". He further instructed her to forward the folder's contents to the File Clerk just once a month for updating. He sent a separate order to the File Clerk, directing him to devote no more than one hour a week to updating addresses, regardless of the presence of a backlog. The VP Admin also issued an order to the marketing director, requiring her department to spot-check the accuracy of the mailing list by randomly calling clients on the list and verifying the contact data. The CEO's original standing order was obscured and, despite all the activity generated by the new orders, little to no progress was made in updating the client database.

---

[6] **arbitraries:** false orders or data entered into a situation or group. They exist or come about seemingly at random or by chance or as an impulsive and unreasonable act of will.

[7] **standing order:** an instruction or prescribed procedure in force permanently or until changed or canceled.

Targets: The Connection to Dev-T

The "targeting" discussed in Chapter 14, *Targeting of Statistics and Quotas*, refers specifically to the actions one should take in order to achieve a quota for his statistic.

In addition to statistical targeting, executives also target the steps of their plans and programs in order to ensure thorough execution and timely completion. The overall target system, i.e., *planning*, consists of the setting of all targets of all types. There are six types of targets. In order to fully understand how the next three items (#10-12) develop traffic, you must become familiar with these two types of targets:

> **Major Target:** the broad general purpose being undertaken, such as "To attain greater security" or "To get the company up to 50 employees."
>
> **Primary Targets:** There is a group of "understood" or continuing targets, called primary targets, which, if overlooked, brings about inaction. These are, in order:
>
> 1. Somebody there
> 2. Worthwhile purpose
> 3. Somebody taking responsibility for the area or action
> 4. Form of the organization[8] planned well
> 5. Form of the organization held or reestablished
> 6. Organization operating
>
> If we have the above "understood" targets, we can go on; BUT IF THESE DROP OUT OR ARE NOT SUBSTITUTED FOR, then no matter what targets are set thereafter they will falter or fail entirely.

10. PRESENT-TIME ORDERS ONLY

Action: Basic programs or standing orders or policy go out by not being enforced.

Result: Present-time orders only are being forwarded or handled. Primary Targets go out. When policy exists but is not made known, random policy setting will occur. Hidden, not-stated random policies can conflict. Illegal policy set at unauthorized levels jams the actions of a group and IS responsible for the inactivity, non-production or lack of team spirit. If we had a game going in which each player set his own rules, there would be no game. There would only be argument and conflict.

---

[8] **form of the organization:** the lines, actions, spaces and flows of an organization, worked out and controlled by employees who are specialists in their respective job functions. These specialists are grouped in departments which have certain actions in common. The departments, having similar functions, are grouped into divisions. The divisions combine into the whole org form. To **hold the form of the org** means seniors ordering the right orders to the right specialists and targeting their production.

An org form is *that arrangement of specialized* <u>terminals</u> *which control and change the production and organization* <u>particles</u> *and flow* <u>lines</u> *of an activity.* **The absence of enforced policy and standing orders and the failure to carry out basic programs through doable targets cause Primary Targets, such as "form of the organization held", to go out. Thus, the terminals, lines and particles eventually become thoroughly entangled and the organization vanishes.**

Example: It was long-standing, written company policy at Mega Corp, a lending firm, that the telemarketers keep an accurate tally of the quantity of phone numbers dialed and contacts made to prospective clients, and that the team manager set weekly quotas for those statistics. There was also a standing order that any phone or mail leads that come into the company would be split evenly among the telemarketers. The company had been experiencing consistent growth for several years when Leo, the recently hired marketing director, decided to make some changes. The first order he issued was to require the telemarketers to keep track of which area codes they dialed and log the number of minutes spent on each call they completed. He told them to concentrate on calling and reaching prospects in affluent areas and to spend at least 15 minutes with each prospect on the phone. He instructed them to not be concerned with the number of prospects they dialed. Leo ordered the team manager to set production quotas for specific area codes. He did not enforce the company quota-setting policy. Leo noticed a dip in the stats that week, so he issued another order to his team manager to give the top telemarketer all the leads, requiring the other telemarketers to do cold calling only. This resulted in low morale and the stats steadily declined for many months thereafter. The form of the organization was not held (Primary Target went out) and one year later, with Leo still in charge of marketing, the company ceased to operate (Primary Target went out). The owner filed for bankruptcy.

11. NONEXISTENT TARGETING

Action: Targets are not set; Major Targets are unknown.

Result: Actions are then unproductive.

Example: Julie, who runs a temporary employment agency, didn't inform her staff that she won the bid to provide the temp help for a new industrial plant opening up in town in two weeks. Her Major Target was to have on hand twenty qualified technicians when the plant opens. Her staff, unaware of this Major Target and having not been given individual targets to fill the plant's needs for technical personnel, continued business as usual, interviewing and hiring only administrative personnel. Those administrative personnel could not be utilized and so the staff's efforts were unproductive.

12. UNREAL TARGETS

Action: Targets which are not derived from any useful Major Target are set and worked on. These targets are "unreal" in that they are not in "agreement" with any Major Target being worked on.

Result: One could have a plan which was targeted — who, when, how — and if the targets were poor or unreal, it would never be completed. One can write a great many targets which have little or nothing to do with the strategic plan and which keep people terribly busy and which accomplish no part of the overall strategic plan.

Example: Steve owns a dry-cleaning business. He has set a Major Target to increase the number of customers by 20% over the next three months. He wrote a series of targets that, when achieved, would accomplish his Major Target. He also wrote a number of targets for his cashier that had nothing to do with the Major Target, including a target to promote and sell a bottle of spot remover to each customer who comes in the door to pick up his clothes. The cashier spent an inordinate amount of time trying to sell the spot remover because she could earn commissions on the sales. Unfortunately, working on this unreal target wasted the time that she could have used to accomplish her other assigned targets, which would have brought in new business. In fact, business declined, most likely because customers found the spot remover to be so effective that they needed fewer clothes dry-cleaned.

13. CROSS TARGETS

Action: **Conflicting targets being set on lower levels.**

Result: **The senior's target system, i.e., planning, is neglected.**

Example: Janet runs a travel agency. She wrote a program to expand her services to include cruises and Hawaiian getaways. She gave very specific targets to each of her travel agents to promote and sell at least 5 cruises and 10 all-inclusive family vacation packages to Hawaii for the next quarter. The office manager, who was given a free spa weekend by a resort owner in the Bahamas, told the agents to make it a priority to promote that resort to each and every one of their clients, and gave them targets to each sell 10 packages during the next quarter. Consequently, the agents neglected Janet's program.

14. BUGGED[9] TARGETS

Action: **A target develops bugs[10] in its forwarding which are not seen or reported.**

Result: **The target stalls. A furious traffic burst may eventually occur to redo it and catch it up.**

Example: Stan is the marketing director at a large investment firm. His company is giving a seminar to 500 prospective clients next Tuesday, just four days from today. The Executive Director assigned his department the project of developing a 45-page color brochure for the seminar attendees and to have 500 copies of it published by Monday, the day before the seminar. Stan completed the design of the brochure last week. He gave his assistant, Art, the target of making 500 copies of the brochure by next Monday. Art planned to make the brochures using the company's high-speed

---

[9] **bugged:** defective.

[10] **bug:** a defect or difficulty.

copier on Sunday, when the office is closed, so that he wouldn't tie up the copier on a workday. On Sunday afternoon, Art showed up at the office and commenced making the copies. He expected the project to take about four hours. After just six copies were made and collated, the copier malfunctioned. The automatic document feeder started to chew up the original pages. Art had to reprint the damaged pages and then hand-feed the document from that point forward, which he estimated would take an additional two hours to complete. Then the collator broke down. Art started to panic. He would now have to hand-collate the entire run of brochures. This would take at least three additional hours. At an estimated nine hours of labor, Art would be in the office until midnight to complete the project. About an hour into his work, one of the color toner cartridges ran out of ink. Art checked the supply room and found that there were no replacement cartridges in stock. As the cartridges are a special order item, Art was unable to complete his task. Rather than report the issue to his boss immediately, Art simply suspended work on the target, assuming his boss would address the bugs in the morning. Stan arrived at work on Monday to find only thirty completed brochures on his desk, with no explanation from Art as to why the target was not done. Art showed up to work late and explained what happened with the copier. The entire marketing department went into action to figure out how to get the brochures copied on such short notice. After dozens of frantic phone calls, they located a copy center 35 miles away that would do the job the same day. It cost the company more than $3,000 and a day's worth of productivity of the entire department to complete the target on time.

---

15. HOBBY-HORSES [11]

Action: An employee can "ride his favorite hobby-horse", ordering and complying only in his favorite area, neglecting areas of greater importance.

Result: His orders often cross-order and distract from important targets and create dev-t, vital actions being neglected.

Example: Rose is the general manager for a high-end cookware store. Her job responsibilities include hiring and firing personnel, floor supervision, establishing the work schedule for 25 associates, setting and monitoring sales quotas, training assistant managers and managing payroll. During the last holiday season, she hired 80 part-time employees to supplement the sales force. One of her favorite duties is to create the work schedule for her staff. While it routinely takes a manager no more than three hours to work out a weekly schedule, Rose spent an entire day at her computer in the back office, painstakingly coordinating everyone's availability and personal schedule preferences. Despite the excessive care taken, Rose inadvertently scheduled some associates to perform functions that didn't match their skill sets. By spending so much time in the back office, she neglected vital actions such as supervision of customer service, driving hourly sales quotas, filling in merchandise on the floor as it sold and managing payroll. She wasn't present to observe that sales were slow and, consequently, she missed the opportunity to send home several of the seasonal employees who were not needed that day.

---

[11] **hobby-horse:** one's favorite topic, idea or project. To **ride a hobby-horse** means to order and comply only in one's favorite area, neglecting areas of greater importance.

16. STALEDATED[12] ORDERS AND MEMOS

Action: Staledating.

Result: It delays action, often important, and creates anxiety and emergencies. New (developed) traffic results in an attempt to get an answer or compliance.

> *Example: On the 5th of June, Kelly, the owner of a gift shop, wrote an order to Paula, her office manager, to inventory the stockroom within three weeks, by the 26th, so that she could review what they had in stock and place an order with her supplier by the 1st of July. It was imperative that the order be placed on the 1st, as the supplier told Kelly that it would take two weeks to process her order, and she needed to restock by the 15th. Paula put the order on her desk, intending to get around to it next week. However, it got buried under a pile of papers in the meantime and Paula forgot all about it. On the 26th, Kelly asked Paula for the inventory sheet. Discovering that Paula hadn't even begun the inventory, they panicked. For the next three days, Kelly was forced to reduce business hours to handle the emergency and complete the inventory in time.*

17. FORMULA EVASION

Action: Areas or persons fail to follow the Conditions formulas assigned or actually indicated and pursue the wrong or no formula.

Result: One will drop down the Conditions without ever understanding why, with consequent ball-up[13] of lines.

> *Example: The month-end sales statistics for a car dealership were nicely up from the previous month, indicating a Normal Condition. Ted, the general manager, decided not to do the steps of the Normal Condition formula because "things are going great; there's no need to waste time writing up a formula and following it." Consequently, he violated the first step of the formula (Don't change anything) by introducing a new operating basis on the sales floor. His sales manager had achieved some success making sales the previous month by taking the prospective buyers on long test-drives. So he issued an order to the sales manager, stating that his sales team must take each person who walks through the door on a long test-drive of the dealership's newest model. There were so many associates out on test-drives that Ted pulled administrative personnel off their jobs to help out on the floor. He even ordered them to take customers on test-drives. This left their positions unattended. Phones rang off the hook, buyers in the financing department were kept waiting and two minor accidents occurred on the test-drives, generating mounds of paperwork for the loss prevention unit. Due to Ted's actions, the lines of the company got all jumbled and confused. Production declined and the Condition by stats dropped to Danger. Ted couldn't understand why it happened.*

---

[12] **staledated, -ing:** The term **staledate** means any memo or answer to a memo that is older in date than one should reasonably expect when he receives it. **Staledating** is the act of causing a written communication or the response to a communication to become a **staledate**. In such instances, the memo or answer to the memo is said to be **staledated**.

[13] **ball-up:** *noun (slang)* utter confusion; a jumbling.

18. INCORRECT CONDITIONS

Action: Incorrect Conditions are assigned or assumed.

Result: Ball-up of lines.

Example: Jason sold five more gym memberships this week than he had during the previous week, yet his senior assigned him a Danger Condition. She erroneously believed that his failure to meet the quota she had set for him was cause to assign him a Danger Condition. Jason applied the Danger Formula when his statistic was actually in a Normal Condition. To spend more time trying to sell memberships, he bypassed his normal routine of coordinating his actions with the marketing director and missed getting some vital information regarding available packages and discounts. He also bypassed his habit of soliciting referrals from new members. Instead, he went off and established a different line with a physical trainer in hopes of generating new sales through her. He also tried to get referrals from a nutritionist. Neither of these actions produced good results. Consequently, he sold fewer memberships the following week and his actual Condition dropped from Normal to Emergency. Sadly, because his statistic dropped and he again failed to meet his quota, his senior will most likely assign him the incorrect Condition, Danger, once again in the coming week. Jason's application of the incorrect Condition formula resulted in a ball-up of his lines. Now he doesn't know which lines to work on to generate new sales for the next week.

19. HAT DUMPING

Action: This is referring everything to someone else.

Result: It greatly increases traffic without producing.

Example: Bradley works after school at the information booth in a large mall. Whenever anyone approaches him to ask the location of a particular store, he immediately refers that person to Mary, the other attendant in the booth, stating that she knows the layout of the mall much better than he does. Consequently, there is, on average, a line of five to ten people waiting to speak with Mary, whose primary duty is to answer incoming phone calls. Many people tire of waiting and leave the booth in frustration, receiving no help, while Bradley idly sits by.

20. CHANNEL[14] SKIPS

Action: Something is not forwarded on channels but skips vital points.

Result: If acted on, confuses the area of the points skipped.

Example: Tom, the office manager, instructed Stan, the company accountant, to propose a budget for the next quarter, without informing Stan's senior, Lucy, the finance director, that he had done so. Earlier, she ordered Stan to conduct an error check on a tax return. Stan didn't know which task had priority and he didn't get

---

[14] **channel:** the proper or official course of transmission of communications. Often used in the plural: *She took her request through official **channels**.*

clarification from Lucy. Instead, he tried to complete both tasks by the deadline and failed. Lucy counted on completion of that task in a timely manner, as she needed to meet an IRS filing deadline. Tom's failure to inform Lucy of his instruction to Stan brought about confusion in her area.

21. VIOLATED PURPOSE

Action: **A division, department, or employee or materiel used for things it was not organized to do.**

Result: **Violation of the division's, department's, employee's or materiel's purpose disrupts its normal lines.**

Example: The owner of a graphic design company purchased a high-speed color printer for his designers to increase productivity. The designers had reported that they were experiencing tremendous delays in completing their work with the old printer. Weeks after the new printer was installed, the owner was dismayed to discover that design production actually declined. Upon closer inspection of the area, he discovered that the personnel in the HR department had tied up the printer with projects ranging from reprinting the company policy manual to printing recruitment flyers and health care benefits packets. Use of the color printer for those items disrupted the lines in the design department.

22. BACKLOGGING

Action: **Traffic or people begin to be backlogged.**

Result: **One can stall completely just handling the queries about the backlog without getting anything really done.**

Example: The hosts of a home shopping network show sold 652 Versa-Mops during a one-hour televised segment. Unfortunately, the fulfillment center had only 60 mops on hand and the remainder on back order. It would be five weeks before the mops would arrive. Consequently, the network's Customer Service call center was deluged for a month with queries from people inquiring about Versa-Mops they had ordered. The call center came to a virtual standstill while addressing this matter, unable to handle the routine traffic from its other televised home shopping programs.

23. OFF-ORIGIN[15] (Statements and Memos)

Action: **An employee originates something not his hat.**

Result: **He creates unnecessary traffic that has to be addressed by the recipient. The recipient would then have to return the communication to the employee, as one does NOT accept a comm that is not the business of the originator's job position.**

---

[15] **off-origin:** *a term designating things originated by a terminal that do not apply to or aren't the business of his job position; a type of dev-t where a terminal originates something not his hat. [Example: an **off-origin** memo would be a memo originated by someone that should have been originated by someone else.]*

Example: Debbie, a vet clinic receptionist, has noticed some of the staff arriving to work as late as 10:00 a.m. Per policy, staff is required to arrive at 8:30. Rather than report her observations to the HR Director, she sent memos to those who have been arriving late, stating that she would report them to HR the next time. Each recipient responded, informing Debbie that he had a modified schedule that was already approved by HR. Further, the HR Director, who received copies of Debbie's memos, had to address the matter as well. He contacted all of the recipients of Debbie's memo and told them to disregard it. He also told Debbie that enforcement of staff work schedules is not her hat and, therefore, her memos were off-origin.

24. OFF-LINE

Action: **Memos or orders are passed in such a way as to deny someone access to information on record[16] which he should have received. A memo is "off-line" when it is sent to the wrong person.**

Result: **The person who is denied access to information he should have received does his job without it. Consequently, he could make poor decisions that adversely affect his production or he might have to redo all his work once he gets access to the data.**

Example: Jenny is the payroll officer for her company. Her job is to calculate and arrange payment of staff salaries and wages. It is standing company policy that any changes to the number of tax exemptions or to health insurance and retirement plan contributions be collected by department heads and submitted directly to Jenny on the first and third Thursday of each month. Last Thursday, Tina, the head of the marketing department, incorrectly forwarded all the payroll change forms that she had collected during the previous two weeks to Brent, her division head. The forms sat in Brent's in-basket for a week before he noticed them. By that time, Jenny had already submitted all the changes to the payroll company for the current pay period. When the payroll checks arrived, six employees were very upset to learn that the changes they requested had not gone into effect. They complained to Margaret, Jenny's supervisor. Upon investigation, Margaret found that Jenny, through no fault of her own, had been denied access to the information in question. She had to retrieve the six payroll checks, submit the changes to the payroll processing company and get the corrected checks issued. This dev-t cost Jenny two hours of her time and involved two other executives needlessly, all because Tina's submission of the payroll information was off-line.

25. INCORRECT ORGANIZATION

Action: **The communications system or procedures are not organized so as to be easily used. They are either not organized at all or are made too complex to be useful.**

Result: **Flowing particles in the organization get restricted, misrouted or halted altogether. Production slows or stops as a result.**

Example: The new office manager of an accounting firm decided to eliminate the position of Communications Director for budgetary reasons. She dismantled the

---

[16] **on record:** (*idiom*) existing as a matter of public knowledge; known.

central comm center, where all staff would go to pick up their incoming phone messages, interoffice memos, etc. Her new communications system was to place a basket on the desk of each executive and require the receptionist to hand-deliver incoming communications once each hour. She further stipulated that there would be just one box located in the lunchroom where the receptionist would place memos and messages for all other employees to sort through. She did away with out-baskets, instead requiring employees and executives alike to personally deliver their interdepartmental communication to the receptionist for further routing. Personnel within the same department would be allowed to deliver memos directly to one another. The office manager devised a "system" that was clearly too complex to be useful and it resulted in inefficiency and less productivity.*

26. ORG BOARD DEV-T

Action: An out-of-date org board.

Result: Causes dev-t.

Action: A staff that doesn't have a well-done org board.

Result: Cannot help but make dev-t.

Action: A staff that doesn't know the org board.

Result: Will make dev-t.

Example: The organizing board for the Phoenix Car Dealership was originally created 15 years ago. The company expanded five years ago to include a used car division with its own separate service center. However, the org board was never updated to reflect that change. Consequently, it appears on the org board that service and maintenance for all cars, new and used, are done in the new car service center. Whenever a customer with a used car comes in for service, the girl at the front desk, following the pattern displayed on the org board, invariably enters the data into the wrong database which adversely affects the marketing division stats, and then routes the customer to the wrong service center, which causes confusion there for both the customer and the mechanic.

27. UNTRAINED STAFF

Action: Employees not grooved in on the lines.

Result: **People in an organization can be working frantically, totally exhausted, and yet produce nothing of value. The reason is that their actions are almost totally dev-t. These people mainly deal in dev-t and, although they even look busy, seldom accomplish much.**

Example: Several new employees were hired to handle an anticipated increase in phone sales at a gift catalog company during the holidays. The supervisor didn't bother to groove in the new staff on how to operate the complex phone system. As a consequence, those new employees inadvertently disconnected many incoming calls. Though at a glance they appeared to be very busy, it was estimated that 25% of the potential holiday revenue was lost.

28. UNPRODUCTIVE PERSONNEL

Action: Retaining an employee who is a flagrant dev-t source.

Result: Morale will be bad because PRODUCTION IS THE BASIS OF MORALE. And who can produce in the midst of disturbances, off-line actions and general dev-t in an area?

Example: Kevin has been the office manager's assistant for nearly a year. During that time there have been more than a dozen separate reports filed on him by virtually every other employee in the company. He has been cited for backlogging his work, hobby-horsing, issuing cross orders, writing false reports, not complying with an order and even misusing the computer to conduct a part-time Internet business. Despite the fact that Kevin is a flagrant source of dev-t and, consequently, company morale is low, Mark, the office manager, has retained him because they're longtime friends and because Mark personally has no problem with Kevin's performance as his assistant.

29. PEOPLE WHO PRESENT PROBLEMS

Action: Problems presented by juniors.

Result: When solved by a senior, they cause dev-t because the source of the problem usually won't use the presented solution either.

Example: Cathy, a telemarketer, was having difficulty using a telephone handset on her job. She explained to her boss that it was a problem for her to hold a handset while writing down information from the customer. She stated that she could be more efficient with hands-free operation. Her boss solved the problem by purchasing a headset for Cathy to use. However, Cathy refused to use the new headset because it wasn't wireless. She explained that she wanted the capability to get up from her desk and walk over to the filing cabinet while talking with the customer.

30. HAVING TO HAVE BEFORE THEY CAN DO

Action: Someone insists he has to have something before he can do something else.

Result: Projects or personal production stall.

Example: When asked why he didn't complete the engineering plans in time to meet with a new client, Jeffrey explained to his boss that he was waiting for delivery of his new drawing board and pens, which he felt he had to have in order to do an acceptable job for his clients.

31. PERMITTING DEV-T

Action: The biggest single goof anyone can make is failing to recognize something as dev-t and going on to handle it anyway.

Result: One's basket soon overflows. The reason for "overwork" and "heavy traffic" is usually traceable to permitting dev-t to exist without understanding it or attempting to put the *dev-t* right.

Example: Gloria, the receptionist at an advertising agency, received a hostile complaint from a client who claimed his consultant gave him poor advice that cost him a great deal of money. He threatened to sue. Not knowing that the proper line for handling dissatisfied clients in the company is to inform Quality Control, Gloria forwarded the matter to her supervisor, Brett, who is the Personnel Director. Being well trained in handling personnel upsets, Brett willingly spent a few hours on the phone with the client and resolved the situation to his satisfaction, avoiding a lawsuit. When Gloria heard the good news, she told fellow employees that if they ever receive a call from an upset or dissatisfied client, they should immediately refer the matter to Brett. In time, Brett's in-basket overflowed with all his unhandled workload, as well as quite a few unhandled customer complaints. He doesn't recognize that routing customer complaints to him is dev-t (off-line), so he doesn't attempt to put it right.

32. LACK OF EXECUTIVE RESPONSIBILITY
"Is this okay?"

Action: Regarding his work, actions or projects, an employee asks his senior, "Is this okay?" The senior, an executive, says that it is.

Result: The senior accepted an "Incomplete Staff Work". He did not meet his executive responsibility to require his junior to forward to him an assembled package of information sufficiently complete to require from him only an "Approved" or "Disapproved". By letting his junior say, "Is this okay?", the executive is now faced with the dev-t of either having to complete the staff work himself or, worse, acting on incomplete data and consequently making a bad and potentially costly decision.

Example: David manages a hotel. Elaine is his assistant. Last week, the facilities manager informed her that one of the four hotel meeting rooms would have to be closed for a month due to renovations, sometime between March 1st and July 31st. Without checking with the events coordinator, Elaine arbitrarily selected May for the renovations. She wrote a memo to David, simply explaining that there would only be three conference rooms available during May due to renovations. She did not provide him with supporting data, such as the events calendar for May, confirmation that there were enough rooms to hold all the scheduled events, etc. She wrote, "Is this okay?" David responded that it was, having assumed that she cleared the dates with the events coordinator. It turned out that all four meeting rooms would be needed in May in order to accommodate events already scheduled. David shirked his executive responsibility — to require a CSW from his junior that states "This is okay." He created much dev-t for himself as a result.

NOTE: Executives may not okay anything done, or to be done, below their level unless their immediate junior has also stated or attested with an initial that it is okay. Never let a junior say "Is this okay?" Always make him state or initial "This is okay" on all work, actions or projects. "Is this okay?" is dev-t and should be reported as such.

33. EXECUTIVE ENTURBULENCE

Action: If an executive is trying to do his or her job and looking ahead and handling things and yet is being hit constantly with bad news and problems and has his in-basket loaded continually, (a) he is getting noncompliance and false reports and (b) his juniors are not getting his orders executed and (c) his juniors are not putting in ethics but leaving it all to him.

Result: The executive's comm lines are jammed; he is threatened by or hit by a catastrophe.

An executive is seldom hit by catastrophe unless he has had noncompliance on his lines. He is almost never hit if he polices[17] dev-t. When an executive is hit by a catastrophe, he should handle it and AT ONCE CHECK UP ON DEV-T AND HANDLE IT. If you find your lines heavy or there is a threatened catastrophe, keep a daily log of dev-t, recording who did what. Then handle the majority offenders.

> *Example: John runs a limousine service in Miami with 24 drivers in his employ. He needed a chauffeur on short notice for a job involving a high-profile VIP client. He chose Gary, who, to John's recollection, has been a reliable employee. He instructed Gary to dress impeccably, arrive early, roll out the red carpet for the client and take him wherever he wants to go for as long as he wants to be there. A few hours later, John received a frantic call from the irate client. He claimed that Gary showed up half an hour late, dressed in jeans and a T-shirt, that he refused to transport one of the people in the client's party without stating a reason, and then drove off leaving the client stranded in the Florida Keys because he was unwilling to work overtime. The client assured John that he would sue him for breach of contract and that he would make sure none of his associates would ever use John's limo service again. Those associates represented 35% of John's business. He handled the flap expeditiously and averted a lawsuit. John then investigated the matter and promptly fired Gary. In the course of his investigation, John found in Gary's personnel file eight separate reports of dev-t. So John could have predicted that Gary was capable of such behavior, had he policed dev-t.*

34. USING DEV-T AS AN EXCUSE TO CUT LINES

Action: Telling someone he is committing dev-t, without really knowing and saying what the exact dev-t was, and then cutting the line because of it.

Result: A cut line (comm line or command line), which consequently impedes the flow of information or particles along that line in the organization.

> *Example: Jack, a sales manager, who directly supervises four sales reps, is responsible for monitoring his juniors' production throughout the day. This morning, he decided to catch up on backlogged paperwork. So he shut his office door, on which he taped a piece of paper with "NO Dev-t, Stay Out Until 3 p.m." written on it. Consequently, three of the sales reps failed to report vital changes to their current sales line-ups. Ellen, the fourth rep, ignored the sign, walked in and told him that she needed to*

---

[17] **police:** to control, regulate or keep in order. One **polices** dev-t by watching for dev-t, spotting it and rapidly getting it off his lines.

speak with him immediately about getting his approval for a deal with a client. Jack promptly snapped back at her, "Dev-t! Get out." He did not say precisely what the alleged dev-t was, nor did he try to handle it. He just wanted to cut the line with Ellen so he could get back to his paperwork. At that point, with the line to her boss cut, she had no idea what to do.

An executive must really know what dev-t is and really say what the exact dev-t was in order to reject or handle dev-t.

35. CATASTROPHES

Action: Periods of excessive dev-t; lack of prediction of a possible circumstance.

Result: Catastrophe [complete failure].

Example: Frank, a restaurant owner, planned an extended trip abroad. He put Lou, the head chef, in charge. Frank gave him a detailed list of tasks to accomplish in addition to handling the day-to-day operations. Lou read the list, which included a directive to ensure that the necessary repairs to the meat refrigerator got done in time for a follow-up inspection by the Health Department, a stack of bills for the bookkeeper to pay and a revised shift schedule for the staff. Lou didn't bother to get the refrigerator repaired (Non Compliance), he changed the shift schedule (Altered Compliance) and never forwarded the bills to the bookkeeper (Non Compliance). Consequently, both the telephone and the electricity were disconnected, two experienced servers quit because they weren't given the hours they had been promised and the restaurant failed the inspection. It was closed by order of the Health Department just two months after Lou took over.

Those things planned for do not become catastrophes. CATASTROPHES USUALLY FOLLOW A PERIOD OF EXCESSIVE DEV-T.

36. ACCEPTING AN ALMOST

Action: Accepting an "almost" compliance, i.e., permitting someone to nearly or partially comply with an order.

Result: The senior must repeat the order more than once before compliance is reported.

Example: Susan is the office manager for a large physical therapy practice located in an office building. The temperature for the entire building is regulated at the Facilities Manager's office. This morning, Susan and her staff arrived to the clinic to find that the thermostat was locked at 80 degrees. She immediately called Steve, the Facilities Manager, and told him to "turn off the heat". An hour later, the heat was still on and the patients were complaining. Susan couldn't reach Steve by phone, so she sent her assistant, Joyce, down to his office to tell him to turn off the heat. When Joyce found Steve, she told him that Susan wants the heat turned off immediately. He responded, "I turned it down a short while ago." Joyce accepted this ALMOST and reported back to Susan, who again had to send Joyce to repeat the directive to "turn off the heat." This time, Joyce returned with the compliance that the heat had been turned off.

An executive or an executive's assistant who accepts and forwards an "almost" is permitting dev-t. Orders given are to be executed and reported DONE, not to be nearly done or almost done. This form of dev-t can often trip up an assistant. In the case of written orders, it is most easily spotted by insisting that the original order or orders be returned with the compliance so that any terminal on the line can tell at a glance *what was ordered* and *what was done*.

37. FAILURE TO GET AN ORDER CLARIFIED

Action: Failing to get an order clarified.

Result: The person receiving the order does something other than what was ordered, or the person's uncertainty about what was ordered gets passed on and perpetuated.

Example: Dale, the owner of a small investment firm wanted to celebrate his company's 10th anniversary and show his appreciation to his clients for their continued loyalty to him by hosting an event that would include a formal dinner and entertainment. There are only 52 active clients, of which Dale anticipated no more than 35 would be able to attend. So he made arrangements for an event for no more than 50 people, including his staff. He ordered his assistant, Sara, to print and send invitations to "all the clients." She was fairly certain that Dale meant to invite every client, both active and inactive, that the company has had during the past ten years. So she sent out 785 invitations. When the RSVP's started coming in, Dale was horrified to find that 392 people accepted the invitation. He had to contact and disinvite all those people who were no longer active clients. This mishap came about simply because Sara didn't get the order to invite "all the clients" clarified. Dale meant "all the active clients." Sara assumed he meant "every client in the database."

38. IRRELEVANT INFORMATION

Action: Providing irrelevant information in response to a question or order. This form of dev-t can also take the form of forwarding large quantities of irrelevant information to a senior.

Result: Jammed lines and reduced productivity of the executive or senior.

Example: Kathleen, an executive at an ad agency, issued a written order to her project manager, Mike, to propose an all-new marketing campaign for The Reynolds Firm, their longtime client. Mike simply wrote back, "The marketing campaign we launched for them two years ago was very effective." That response had nothing to do with launching a new campaign. Kathleen reissued the order to Mike. While he acknowledged the order appropriately that time, he also forwarded to her, without being told to do so and without explanation, several boxes of surveys used in the previous campaign. Kathleen spent an hour going through the boxes of material before she realized the contents were outdated surveys, completely useless for the new campaign. By forwarding irrelevant information, Mike jammed Kathleen's lines and caused her to lose production time.

39. REASONABLENESS

Action: **An employee or executive can be "reasonable" and accept reasons why something cannot be done, accept incomplete cycles of action as complete, and fail to follow through and get completions.**

Result: **All these result in further traffic.**

Example: Candice owns and operates a flower shop. She had a contract to provide the flowers for a wedding, which is to take place on Saturday. The bride wants her bouquet to contain some very rare orchids, which could only be purchased from a supplier in Bixby, a town 30 miles away. Candice instructed her assistant, Donna, to make sure the orchids were available and picked up by Friday. On the day Donna was supposed to pick up the flowers, she told Candice she couldn't drive to Bixby because she was having car trouble. Candice told her she could drive the company car. Donna said she didn't want to go because she might get lost. Candice provided her with a detailed map and directions. Finally, Donna said she didn't want to go because it might rain and she is afraid to drive in the rain. Candice gave in and ended up driving to Bixby herself.

Candice could have rejected all of Donna's excuses for not doing her job and, instead, told her to MAKE IT GO RIGHT.

Knowing and applying the following datum best handles this form of dev-t:
THE SUPREME TEST OF A PERSON IS HIS ABILITY TO MAKE THINGS GO RIGHT.

40. FAILURE TO HANDLE SITUATIONS TO CONCLUSION; REFERRAL

Action: **Refusal to take responsibility for ending a situation; continuing a situation by referring it to someone else.**

Result: **You can develop more traffic internally, more upsets and more ARC breaks than anything you can mention.**

Example: The water fountain in the reception area of a dental office had been leaking for two weeks. At first, the receptionist mopped up the puddle, but she took no further action to get the fountain repaired. After two weeks of daily mopping and when noticing the increasing rate of the leak, the receptionist reported the matter to the leasing office. However, the landlord did not feel it was his responsibility to handle because the water fountain belonged to the dental practice. No one took action and a week later, one of the patients slipped and fell in the puddle. She filed a personal injury lawsuit shortly thereafter. A week after that, the pipe supplying water to the fountain burst in the middle of the night, flooding the dental practice and the offices on the floor below. The dentist and the landlord are no longer on speaking terms. The cost, in terms of property damage, was more than $25,000. They have been fighting in court for several months over who is liable.

The only tremendous error an organization makes, next to "inspection before the fact",[18] is failing to rapidly handle situations to conclusion. The fault of an organization's waffle,[19] waffle, waffle, "Joe won't take responsibility for it", "It's got to go someplace else", and all that sort of thing, is that it *continues* a situation. What you should specialize in is terminating a situation, not referring it to someone else. If the situation comes up in your vicinity, well, handle it — that is, finish it off so that is the end of it. So what you ought to do is *complete the action* now, in the first place.

41. FAILURE TO COMPLETE A CYCLE OF ACTION, AND REFERRAL

Action: Failing to complete a cycle of action by deferring it for completion later. [Example: You pick up a memo or a piece of work, look it over and then put it aside to do later, then later you pick it up and read it again and only then do you do it.]

Result: This doubles your traffic.

Action: Referring the cycle of action to someone else. [Example: You receive a request for information about something in your area; you're busy, so you forward it to someone else who you later learn didn't have the data that was requested.]

Result: Everything you refer has to be done when it comes back to you.

> *Example: Perry is the editor of a local newspaper. He wanted to publish a story, a "then & now" piece, about a historic mansion in town, which is celebrating its bicentennial. He gave the assignment to Clark, his ace reporter. When Clark received the memo, he realized he would have to research the history of the mansion. He doesn't particularly enjoy doing research of this type, so he passed it off to Jimmy, an intern, to do for him. Several days later, Jimmy gave Clark a handful of brochures about the mansion and a pamphlet about ghosts who roam its halls. Clark realized he would have to do the research himself. He scheduled it in his calendar to do the next week. He postponed the task several more times, all the while reassuring Perry that he was working on it. By the time he got around to actually writing it, the deadline had passed and Perry rejected the article entirely and gave Clark a formal reprimand. Clark spent nearly a month trying to avoid writing an article that might have taken him a couple of days to complete.*

42. FAILURE TO RECORD AN ORDER

Action: An executive fails to make an adequate record of an order given; the recipient loses or misplaces the order.

Result: This can result in endless dev-t. Due to the original orders being lost or not recorded at all, wrong items are purchased, incorrect actions are taken, cross orders are given and a tremendous waste of executive time and money occurs straightening the matter out.

This is one of the most serious sources of dev-t.

---

[18] **inspection before the fact:** inspection before anything bad has happened.

[19] **waffle: 1.** to pause or hold back in uncertainty or unwillingness. **2.** to be unable to make a decision; vacillate.

Example: Pete, the Marketing Director for a company that manufactures novelty products, wrote an order to Rick, his team leader, to conduct a very specialized survey of 500 parents of children between the ages of 5 and 10 to determine how best to market and advertise their newest board game. The company manufactured a quantity of 10,000, in anticipation of upcoming holiday sales. Pete gave Rick a deadline of November 1st, a period of three weeks, to furnish the much needed survey data. In the interim, Rick lost the order and subsequently forgot about doing the survey. To make matters worse, Pete never made a record of the order and, with nothing in writing to jog his memory, he never followed up with Rick to see that it got done. On November 1st, Pete's boss asked him how the marketing of the new board game was coming along. At that moment, he remembered the order he gave Rick and that's when he learned that Rick never conducted the survey. It was too late to do one in-house, so he outsourced the job to a marketing firm that charged double their usual rates to complete the surveys in 72 hours. The promotional materials created using the survey results from the outside company did not have the hoped-for impact on board game sales. When the holidays were over, the company was left with 8,500 board games in their inventory and, due to the cost of the outsourcing, the company experienced a net loss of $5,000.

43. UNCLEAR ORDERS

Action: An executive gives an unclear order.

Result: He puts uncertainty and confusion on the line right at the very beginning of the cycle of command.

Example: Celia, the regional manager of Commerce Bank, wanted to increase the number of new signature loans for the quarter. She allocated funds for a promotional action. She wrote the following order to her tellers: Commerce Bank will pay $50 for every new account. The tellers argued among themselves about what the order meant. Some tellers understood it to mean that they would receive $50 for each loan they got a customer to take out. Other tellers thought it meant that customers would receive $50 for opening a checking account. Since there was no deadline date, some tellers were promising customers $50 as long as they open an account this year. Several weeks into the campaign, Celia learned of the confusion her order had created and the resultant financial loss for the bank. She should have written the order as follows: For every approved new signature loan account, in the amount of $7,500 or more, opened by a customer between the 1st of May and the 30th of June, Commerce Bank will credit the account $50 toward the first month's interest payment.

44. MISUNDERSTOOD ORDERS

Action: A junior misunderstands an order.

Result: Orders misunderstood by the recipient will not be properly complied with, as the order was misunderstood. The incorrect or no action that follows will require further traffic to correct.

Example: The Chief Information Officer at a magazine publishing company wrote the following order to the Network Administrator: Purge all the duplicate records in the customer database and those that contain bogus addresses. Not entirely sure what the CIO meant by "duplicate" records and "bogus" addresses, the network administrator deleted all the records of customers in the database whose names had been entered more than once, i.e., including the original records, and all records that contained two addresses for the same person.

As an executive, originate clear, precise instructions and orders. As a junior, duplicate the order, and never fail to clarify if you feel you might have misunderstood.

45. RELAYING AN ORDER IN A CONFUSING MANNER

Action: Assistants and secretaries relay orders or information poorly.

Result: They can create dev-t and foul up actions.

Example: The owner of a general contracting firm told his assistant to have the foreman inspect the hotel job site and give him a <u>progress report</u> on it by the end of the day. The assistant texted the foreman, telling him that the owner wanted to know <u>what's going on</u> at the hotel job site. The foreman became alarmed, thinking that there must be some sort of an emergency. He immediately left another job site that required his presence and went to the hotel job site. He found everything to be in order and on schedule. In the meantime, work at the other site came to a complete halt when the concrete company failed to show up to pour the foundation.

46. CLEANING CLEANS

Action: Doing something that is already done or ordering something to be done that has already been done.

Result: Double work. Unnecessary traffic.

Example: Angie is a student who interns for a photographer. This morning, he left written instructions for her to print the photos that he shot for the Davis-Martin wedding. Angie wonders why he needs a second set, as she has already completed that task. Rather than informing him she had already done it, she prints a second set.

47. REPEATED TRAFFIC

Action: The same traffic repeated to the same executive. It often takes the form of information or compliance reported by one means of communication and then the *same* information being sent by another means.

Result: Unnecessary traffic that eats up an executive's time and patience.

Example: Veronica is a paralegal in an attorney's office. Early this morning, she sent her supervisor an e-mail detailing the current status of a case she is researching for him. Shortly after lunch, she walks into his office, interrupting a phone consultation, and commences to explain virtually everything she wrote in her e-mail.

48. FAILURE TO WEAR YOUR HAT

Action: **A person in one job position not doing that job but doing every other job.**

Result: **It creates endless dev-t, in that all memos and originated communication are off-origin and he is camouflaging the hole of his own job. The person himself is the dev-t.**

> *Example: Bobbi is the Executive Director for a consulting firm. Her primary duties are to ensure the company attains and maintains solvency through ample income and delivery of service, to supervise the senior executives, to write strategic plans for the company and to ensure they are successfully carried out. However, at any given moment during the workday, Bobbi can be found doing anything but her job duties. She likes to consult clients and so she has taken over delivering service to some of them herself; she likes to sell services, so she spends time with the salesmen to show them how to do it "the right way"; she handles dissatisfied clients because the customer service department is "too busy" to handle the traffic; she even covers reception when the receptionist is on lunch break. Bobbi appears on the surface to be helping the company in many ways, but she is confusing the proper lines in the company, originating memos from positions that are not hers. As for the duties of her own job, well, they're not getting done and Bobbi is covering that up by appearing busy throughout the company. She herself is the dev-t.*

49. UNUSUAL SOLUTIONS

Action: **Requests for authorization to depart from the usual. Juniors who propose unusual solutions generally don't know the policy or orders anyway.**

Result: **Such requests are dangerous when okayed, as they then set up areas of difference and cause policy to fall out of use.**

The proper thing to do is order a checkout[20] on the appropriate policy.

> *Example: Brad is the top salesman for an electronics store. It was the last day of the quarter and he was doing everything he could to make his sales quota and earn a hefty quarterly bonus. He had been cultivating a prospect, a friend, who was finally ready to buy a $3,000 state-of-the-art TV, but wouldn't have the funds for another week. Brad asked his supervisor for permission to put the charge on his own credit card so he could earn the bonus, despite the fact that company policy expressly forbids counting purchases made by an employee as a qualified sale in the bonus incentive program. The supervisor okayed the request "just this once" to help Brad earn the bonus. The rest of the sales staff found out about the deal and wanted to know why Brad got to do it and they couldn't; they accused their boss of playing favorites. Brad reached his quota because of that purchase and he earned his bonus. However, a week later, the customer returned the TV. Brad reluctantly had to pay back his $1,500 bonus. His coworkers are resentful at the special treatment Brad received and the supervisor now has a store full of sales reps with low morale.*

---

[20] **checkout:** (*noun*) the action of verifying a person's knowledge of something, particularly an item given on a checksheet. [Example: *The training officer ordered a* **checkout** *of the materials John studied today.*]

50. REMOVING PARTICLES OFF THE LINE

Action: Taking communication particles off another's desk or out of his in-basket or off the communication lines.

Result: Apart from being a serious offense, it causes dev-t and lost time in searching for the missing particles and can sabotage projects or actions because vital data is missing.

Example: Kristin is a file clerk for a prominent consulting firm. The company has set up a basket in which the staff may put particles to be filed. It is Kristin's job to file those particles in the appropriate client folders in the filing cabinet. If a client folder is missing from the cabinet, Kristin is supposed to check the sign-out log to locate it, file the particle in the folder and leave the folder precisely where she found it. Last week, Kristin decided to collect up all the client folders for which she had particles to file and do the filing at her desk. No one knew she had done this. To make matters worse, Kristin left the office early that afternoon to handle a personal matter. Around that same time, the consultants were about to contact their clients for their scheduled phone calls. However, they discovered that the folders containing all the data about the clients' businesses were missing. They became frantic. They started running from office to office, asking anyone and everyone if they had seen a particular folder. No one knew where they were and Kristin, who had taken them, was gone for the day. The consultants had to call their clients and reschedule the appointments. Several executives had to join in an office-wide search for the folders, which were ultimately found in Kristin's desk drawer. She was severely reprimanded.

51. SLOW COMM LINES

Action: Memos held up on lines.

Result: It causes other memos to be originated about the same subject, causing dev-t to both sender and recipient.

Example: Molly, the office manager for a prestigious law firm, sent a memo via the supply officer to the purchaser regarding the coffee service for the clients. She wanted to let Blake, the purchaser, know that the coffee and bottled water consumption rate has apparently increased markedly. She directed that a double order be placed for the next month and requested acknowledgment of receipt of the memo. Two weeks passed and she had yet to receive a reply. She sent another memo directly to Blake demanding to know what was taking him so long to acknowledge her first memo. When he received the second memo this morning, he called her and explained he just received the first memo yesterday and that he didn't see the urgency in responding, as the order for next month had already been placed and delivered, so it was too late to double the order. Upon inspection of the first memo, Molly discovered that the supply officer signed off on it 12 days after Molly put it in his basket.

The power of an organization is directly proportional to its speed of particle flow (letters, memos, people, etc.).

Chapter 20

HOW TO HANDLE WORK

DO IT NOW.

One of the best ways to cut your work in half is not to do it twice. Probably your most fruitful source of dev-t is your own double work.

This is the way you do double work: You pick up a memo or a piece of work, look it over and then put it aside to do later; then later you pick it up and read it again and only then do you do it. This of course doubles your traffic just like that.

Make it a firm rule that when you find yourself handling a piece of traffic, you *handle* it. Don't put it into your *pending* basket, unless it cannot be dealt with immediately. If you are given a message or a datum (a piece of information) that requires further action from you, do it right when you receive it, whenever possible. This is how you buy "loafing time".

There's no need to look busy if you are not busy. There is no need to fondle and caress work because there isn't enough of it. There's plenty of work to do. The best answer to work of any kind is to do it.

If you do every piece of work that comes your way WHEN it comes your way and not after a while, if you always take the initiative and take action, not refer it, you never get any traffic back.

In short, the way to get rid of traffic is to do it, not to refer it; anything referred has to be read by you again, digested again, and handled again; so never refer traffic, just do it so it's done.

You can keep a communication line in endless foment[1] by pretending that the easiest way not to work is to not handle things or to refer things. Everything you don't handle comes back and bites. Everything you refer has to be done when it comes back to you.

So if you are truly a lover of ease, the sort of person who yawns comfortably and wears holes in heels resting them on desks, if your true ambition is one long bout of spring fever,[2] then you'll handle everything that comes your way when it comes and not later; and you'll never refer anything to anybody that you yourself can do promptly.

---

[1] **foment:** (*noun*) state of excitation.

[2] **spring fever:** the laziness or restlessness that many people feel during the first warm, sunny days of spring.

Ethics

Chapter 21

THE DESIGN OF ETHICS

In order to understand the role of *ethics* in an organization, we must first understand what *ethics* is and what its relationship is to *morals* and *justice*.

In the modern dictionary we find that *ethics* are defined as "morals" and *morals* are defined as "ethics". These two words are *not* interchangeable.

MORALS should be defined as **a code of good conduct laid down out of the experience of a culture or society to serve as a uniform yardstick for the conduct of individuals and groups.** Morals are actually laws. The origin of a moral code comes about when it is discovered through actual experience that some act is more non-survival than pro-survival. The prohibition of this act then enters into the customs of the people and may eventually become a law.

Example: The first half of the 20th Century saw periods of prohibition of alcoholic beverages in seven countries, including the United States and Russia. In the United States, the movement to prohibit production and consumption of alcohol found most of its support in women who were opposed to the domestic violence associated with alcohol abuse, and the large share of household income it could consume, which was especially burdensome to the low-income working class. Consequently, it was determined to be more non-survival than pro-survival to permit the consumption of alcohol, and Prohibition went into effect in 1920. As Prohibition became increasingly unpopular during the Great Depression that began in 1929, especially in large cities, "Repeal" was eagerly anticipated. The consumption of alcohol, considered more non-survival than pro-survival prior to the Depression, was deemed more pro-survival by the fourth year of the Depression. The Eighteenth Amendment to the US Constitution (Prohibition) was repealed with ratification of the Twenty-first Amendment in 1933.

In the absence of extended reasoning powers, moral codes, so long as they provide better survival for their group, are a vital and necessary part of any culture.

ETHICS, on the other hand, are **the rules or standards governing the conduct of a person** (*personal ethics*) **or the conduct of the members of a profession** (e.g., *business ethics* or *medical ethics*). Ethics actually consists of rationality toward the highest level of survival for the individual, the group, mankind and the other dynamics taken up collectively. Ethics are reason. Ethics are the actions an individual takes on himself in order to accomplish optimum survival for himself and others on all dynamics. It is a personal thing. It is a First Dynamic action.

Example: Dan has been under a lot of stress on the job lately. His workload has grown to nearly twice what it used to be, but he hasn't said a word to his boss. He doesn't want to be perceived as incapable or as a whiner. Instead, Dan dealt with the stress by drowning it in alcohol. While he occasionally drinks wine with dinner, his consumption of alcohol has significantly increased during the past few months. He has been frequenting a bar on the way home almost every night. His wife, Jenny, has noticed a dramatic change in his attitude toward her and the kids. He has clearly developed a drinking problem. Jenny brought the matter to his attention. At first he dismissed her concerns. However, upon reflection, he admitted to himself that his job performance was slipping, which added to his stress; he had gained quite a bit of weight and felt very sluggish as a result; and he had become short-tempered with his children. Dan didn't like what was happening to him, so he decided to stop the downward spiral. He reviewed the First Dynamic Danger Formula and saw how he could apply it to his situation. He immediately quit drinking altogether and he directly confronted the source of his stress. He spoke with his supervisor at work and got him to agree to lessen Dan's workload. He even gave Dan a part-time assistant to help with his backlogged work. Dan apologized to his wife and kids for his recent behavior and made up the damage he caused to his relationships with them. He even started working out on a regular basis to get back into shape. Dan felt great having regained control of his life and dynamics.

When one is ethical or "has his ethics in", it is by his own determination. He himself takes the actions to be ethical. In other words, he puts his own ethics in; he and his actions are said to be *in-ethics*. Conversely, by *out-ethics* we mean an action or situation in which an individual is involved, or something the individual does, which is contrary to the ideals, best interests and survival of his dynamics.

If a moral code were thoroughly reasonable, it could, at the same time be considered thoroughly ethical. But only at this highest level could the two be called the same. Ethical conduct includes the adherence to the moral codes of the society in which we live.

JUSTICE is **the action taken on the individual by the group when he fails to get his own ethics in**, i.e., when he fails to take the actions that would accomplish optimum survival for himself and others. *Justice* means fair and equitable treatment for both the group and the individual.

Justice would consist of a refusal to accept any report not substantiated by actual, independent data, seeing that all such reports are investigated and that all investigations include confronting the accused with the accusation and where feasible the accuser, BEFORE any disciplinary action is undertaken or any Condition assigned.

To achieve that end, companies have a department called "Inspections and Reports", or I&R, which is located in the Human Resources Division. There are two sections within I&R: the Inspections Section, run by the Inspections Officer, and the Ethics Section (simply referred to as Ethics), run by the Ethics Officer. In small companies, there is usually just one person in the I&R Department; he would wear the hats of both the Inspections and Ethics Officers.

INSPECTIONS OFFICER

The basic duties of the Department of I&R are what it says: *inspections and reports*. The duty of the Inspections Officer is to inspect the status of various projects and orders and report this to the head of the division concerned. Inspecting and reporting alone usually work.

The Inspections Officer monitors the company's statistic graphs and conducts inspections into areas where statistics are down in order to ascertain *why* they are down. He reports his findings to the senior executives of the company for further action by them. When an employee is not doing his job well or at all, as evidenced by down-trending statistics, the Inspections Officer assists him by doing a full inspection of the area in which he works as an attempt to remedy the situation. The intention of this inspection is to HAT,[1] DON'T HIT personnel, meaning put hats on them, don't try to solve it with ethics. The lazy action is to assign a Condition. The more sensible action is to fully inspect and attempt to remedy.

When this doesn't work and stats fall or people fall off the org board, e.g., when employees quit abruptly or are terminated unjustly (situations that are often observed in work environments where job security is uncertain), one goes into *ethics actions*.[2] WHEN inspection reveals outness,[3] and reports (such as graphs or information submitted by the Inspections Officer to the senior executives) do not result in correction, THEN it is a matter for the Ethics Section. Ethics should only be used as an extreme last resort.

ETHICS OFFICER

Upon notification by the Inspections Officer that an individual or area continues to have fallen stats, down-trending stats or false stats, or if one fails to report stats altogether, the Ethics Officer conducts an investigation into the affected area and takes the disciplinary actions that are called for and prescribed by company policy to eliminate the demonstrated counter-efforts[4] to the organization's stated goals.

One of the primary functions of the Ethics Officer is to support and protect employees who are doing their jobs well (i.e., they have up-trending statistics). He does this by ensuring they apply the correct weekly Condition formula for their statistics. He also employs a

---

[1] **hat:** (*verb*) to instruct a person in the proper performance of one or more aspects of his job. [Example: *The first action Dave took to improve his department's customer service feedback score was to **hat** his juniors on proper phone etiquette.*]

[2] **ethics actions:** any disciplinary measures taken with an employee to address and remove demonstrated counter-intentions from the environment. *Counter-intention* means a determination to follow a goal which is in direct conflict with that known to be the goal(s) of the group.

[3] **outness:** a deviation from what is accurate or right; something in disagreement or at variance with the correct procedures or optimum conditions in an organization. [Example: *Not using the proper procedure to route incoming phone calls, resulting in calls being lost, is an **outness**.*] To be a good executive or employee, one has to know the right way something is done and to be able to apply and get done what he knows and be able to correct **outnesses** so they go back to the correct procedure.

[4] **counter-effort:** a determined attempt to do something in opposition to someone or some thing. [Example: *Refusing to keep track of his statistics on a daily basis was Josh's **counter-effort** to his senior's requirement to keep a daily graph of his production.*]

system of rewards and penalties. He makes certain that upstats[5] are rewarded for their contributions to the production of their sections, their departments and the organization as a whole.

He ensures that downstats[6] properly apply the appropriate Condition formula so that their statistics begin to rise. Further, he sees that low production and downstats are penalized, not rewarded, in accordance with established company policy.

Ethics only exists to hold the fort long enough and settle things down enough to get technology in. Ethics is never carried on for its own sake. The Ethics Officer carries on with his investigations and ethics actions only until the individual employee's statistics are up-trending and his job is being performed properly. The Ethics Officer's primary goal is to facilitate the company's expansion and ensure its future survival. He does this by getting ethics in and keeping it in.

---

[5] **upstat:** one who has high personal production statistics. An **upstat** group would be a group whose overall production statistics are high.

[6] **downstat:** one who has low or declining personal production statistics. A **downstat** group would be a group whose overall production statistics are low or declining.

Chapter 22

REWARDS AND PENALTIES
A System For Achieving Productivity

Employees *are* expected to do their jobs and there are no excuses at all for not doing so. The subject of what one receives in return for contributing is as variable as the desires of man.

REWARDS

Rewards are not necessarily proportional to one's contribution and do not necessarily establish the degree of contribution. Actually a "reward" is what one desires, not what is given.

Approval and validation are often far more valuable than material rewards and are usually worked for far harder than mere pay. Even being part of an important team is a return contribution. Thus, "customer approval" of the team is part of the rewards one achieves.

PENALTIES

When a state of discipline does not exist, the whole group caves in. It has been noted continually that the failure of a group began with a lack of or a loss of discipline. Without it, the group and its members perish. One can't expect them to fall all over a goofing employee whose lack of performance upsets the lines and production. It does far more harm than good to let the situation continue without taking action.

Therefore, a code of discipline needs to be established, made plain for everyone to see, with limits against overpunishment and recourse for those who are wronged. Accordingly, this code of offenses and their penalties should become firm and expressed policy. Most often, this policy takes the form of a "Code of Conduct".

Lack of specified offenses, penalties and recourse bring everyone to uncertainty and risk at the whim of those in charge.

THE SYSTEM

This seemingly obvious law is important to grasp:

Natural Law: WHEN YOU REWARD DOWN-STATISTICS AND PENALIZE UP-STATISTICS, YOU GET DOWN-STATISTICS.

If you reward nonproduction, you get nonproduction.

When you penalize production, you get nonproduction.

In the conduct of your affairs in all matters of rewards and penalties, pay sharp heed to the basic laws as above and use this policy: **Award production and up-statistics and penalize nonproduction and down-statistics.** Always.

Also, do it *all* by statistics—not rumor or personality or who knows who. And make sure everyone has a statistic of some sort.

Promote by statistic only. Penalize down-statistics only. *Never* promote a downstat or demote an upstat.

It might seem odd that an executive would penalize production. Unfortunately, it happens. And if it should happen to you, don't let your supervisor's error affect you adversely. Show him your stats and point out that you should be rewarded, not penalized.

And if your stats are down and your boss rewards you despite that fact, do the right thing and bring this to his attention. There is the matter of exchange. If your stats are down, you've done nothing to deserve a reward. You know it and, chances are, your fellow employees know it and they will resent you for accepting unearned rewards. Do your part to foster team spirit and good morale.

SUMMARY

Ethics actions are often used to handle down-statistics of the individual employee. A person who is not doing his job becomes the focus of investigation by Ethics. Conversely, if a person *is* doing his job (and his statistic will show that), ethics is considered to be *in* and the person is *protected* by Ethics. One can get away with murder[1] so long as he is a producing, high-statistic employee.

It is very easy for an employee to completely misunderstand ethics and its functions. Due to past bad experiences, one is likely to identify any justice action or symbol of justice (such as a judge or a policeman) with oppression. Yet in the absence of true ethics, no one can live with others and stats go down inevitably.

It is *not* humanitarian to let a *whole* population go to pieces just because a few refuse to work. And some people just won't. And when work no longer has reward, none will. So specialize in production and everybody wins. Reward it.

---

[1] **get away with murder:** (*figurative expression*) to commit an act for which one could incur strong disapproval or harsh criticism without being punished.

Chapter 23

ETHICS REPORTS

To succeed in this "civilization" or *any* society, crude or sophisticated, one has to act continually to keep one's own environment under some control. It *does* matter what goes on around one. The only thing which does not care is a corpse.

It is a rather simple thing—not heroic. If one can't control a coffee cup he is likely to get scalded! If one can't control a car he is a statistic. Extend this to one's coworkers slightly and it is plain to see that total permissiveness is suicide. Standing with a bland look while Joe sticks pins in someone or something is not good manners, it's idiocy!

To live at all, one has to exert some control over his equals as well as his juniors and (believe it or not) his superiors. When misconduct and out-ethics is occurring in a group, it is almost impossible for other members of the group not to know of it. At least some of them are aware of the outness.

When a group has down stats, it is not true that *all* of them are trying to fail. Only a few are dedicated to not doing their jobs. The question one can ask of any group that is not doing well is this: Why did the *other* group members tolerate and ignore the loafers or out-ethics people in it?

There is ONE factor which makes an upstat group upstat and a downstat group downstat and a horror to be around. The single most notable difference between an upstat, easy-to-live-and-work-with group and a downstat, hard-to-live-and-work-with group is that the individual group members themselves enforce the action and mores[1] of the group. *That* is the difference—no other.

In an upstat group, at the first pinprick Joe would probably have a black eye! In a downstat group Joe could go on and on with his pins, each group member watching and shrugging. In a group where members have some concept of controlling their environment and their fellows, you don't have loafers or out-ethics people—*because* the rest of the group, on an individual basis, just won't tolerate it. Those who would have a tendency to wreak havoc[2] or loaf don't dare. And the group becomes easy to live with and work with.

So, if one were seeking the key factor that makes a group easy to live and work with, it is not whether individuals in the group should be preselected or carefully made ethical by some process or by inspired leadership. It is whether the group members themselves exert any control on each other.

---

[1] **mores:** (pronounced ***mor·aze***) the customs and manners of a social group or culture. **Mores** often serve as moral guidelines for acceptable behavior but are not necessarily religious or ethical.

[2] **wreak havoc:** to bring about or cause disorder or chaos.

Examples of group members *not* exerting control on each other:

> *"If I report the sales manager for violating policy, the executive director would fire me—she's his wife!"*

> *"If I complain that management won't let me wear my hat, they'll take disciplinary action against me for spreading 'lies' about them."*

If such conditions prevail, the group has already lost the group ability to control the environment—and they will be downstat. Their pay will be low—their working conditions rotten.

There is a mechanism to prevent this. It is called *Ethics Reports*.

A person with knowledge of nonoptimum conduct by other group members must write the report and file it with the Ethics Officer.

Ethics Reports may be written on matters such as:

- Any damage to anything, noting the name of the person in charge of it (DAMAGE REPORT)

- The misuse or abuse of any equipment or materiel, meaning using it wrongly or for a purpose not intended (MISUSE REPORT)

- The waste of company materiel (WASTE REPORT)

- The idleness of equipment or personnel which should be in action (IDLE REPORT)

- The disappearance or theft of company or personal property (LOSS or THEFT REPORT)

- Noncompliance with valid orders (NONCOMPLIANCE REPORT)

- Dev-t (DEV-T REPORT) [NOTE: If an employee routinely experiences dev-t, he should keep a dev-t log and write down the name of anyone he is getting dev-t from and also report in writing to Ethics any violation of company policy regarding dev-t.]

- Job Endangerment (JOB ENDANGERMENT REPORT)[3]

- Knowledge of any loafing or destructive or off-policy or out-ethics action, or on noting some investigation is in progress and having data on it of value to Ethics (KNOWLEDGE REPORT)

The report form is simple. It is a memo addressed simply to the Ethics Officer. It is dated. It has under the address and in the center of the page the name of the person or portion of the organization reported on. It then states what kind of report it is. The original goes to Ethics by drawing an arrow pointing to "Ethics Officer" and the copy goes to the person or portion of the organization being reported on *by channels*.[4]

---

[3] **Job Endangerment Report:** an Ethics Report that one files on his next highest superior in the event that he is given orders or directions or preventions or denied materials which make it hard or impossible for him to raise his statistics or do his job at all. While a **Job Endangerment Report** may be filed on anyone (superiors, equals or juniors), it is normally filed on a direct senior who has issued an order that endangered one's job by demanding one alter or depart from known policy.

[4] **by channels:** A command **channel** is a type of communication routing. Command **channels** go up through seniors, over to a senior and down to a junior. Or they go up through all seniors. It is used upward for unusual permission, authorizations, information, important actions or compliances. Downward it is used for orders. An Ethics Report routed **"by channels"** means that it is sent by the originator up through his seniors, over to the senior of the person named in the report and down to the recipient. [See definition of **command channel** in the glossary on page 168 for an illustration of a report routed **by channels**.]

The originator indicates with an arrow the first destination. Each *via* on the channel routing (1) initials, (2) dates and (3) forwards the report to the next hat (job position) in the routing by indicating with an arrow the next destination.

SAMPLE ETHICS REPORT

> To: *Ethics Officer* Date: Dec 18
> cc: *Receptionist* ←
> via: *Personnel Mgr* ← DB 12/20
> via: *Sales Manager* ← BJ 12/19
>
> From: Customer Service Rep
>
> **Helen Chapman**
> Dev-t Report
>
> *Helen Chapman, receptionist, took a phone message for me from a prospective client yesterday afternoon at 3:00. He told her that he couldn't make our scheduled appointment at his office early the next morning. Helen left for the day without delivering that message to me. So I went to meet him at 7:00 this morning as planned, and upon arrival I was told that he had cancelled the appointment with Helen yesterday. When I got back to the office, the message was still on her desk.*
>
> *I wasted two hours on the road and missed several important calls by being out of the office this morning. This is the third time in the past two weeks that I've reported Helen for staledating important messages.*
>
> *— David Lange*

THINGS THAT SHOULDN'T BE

If you see something going on in your organization or something incorrect that you don't like and yet do not wish to turn in an ethics report, or indeed don't know whom to report, WRITE A MEMO TO THE INSPECTIONS OFFICER. Tell him what you have noticed and give him what data you can. You can entitle the memo, "Things That Shouldn't Be Report."

The Inspections Officer will then investigate it and make a report to the right executives or turn in an ethics report on the offending persons himself.

Don't just natter (grumble or gossip) if there is something you don't like. Tell the Inspections Officer. Then something can be done about it.

DISPUTED ETHICS REPORTS

When one receives an ethics report that he feels is incorrect, the answer is not to issue another report naming the person that issued the first report. Such action merely sets up a vicious circle of ethics reports going between two persons.

If anyone receives an ethics report, he should first take a good look at his actions and see what needs to be done in order to avoid a repetition of the offense. If, however, after careful consideration he considers the report really unjustified, he should send a polite memo to the Ethics Officer, stating briefly his reasons, supported where possible with data and ask for the report to be withdrawn. If, in light of the data received, Ethics is satisfied that the report was incorrectly issued, he can return the report and explanation to the originator asking for the report to be withdrawn. If the originator decides now to withdraw the report after seeing the explanation, he returns it to Ethics requesting cancellation and Ethics removes the report from the file.

If the originator is dissatisfied with the explanation, the report should not be withdrawn. The originator sends the memo and report back to the Ethics Officer with "To Ethics—File" written on it. Ethics informs the receiver and files. In this case, the receiver can, if he wishes, appeal by memo to the Ethics Officer and ask for a hearing. Thereupon, the Ethics Officer calls both the originator and the receiver to his office and, taking only the facts set out in the receiver's memo to Ethics, makes a quick investigation.

The Ethics Officer then makes one of the following adjudications:

1. Have the ethics report destroyed.
2. Have the ethics report destroyed and if he finds that the report was carelessly or incorrectly issued (bearing in mind what information was available to the originator at the time of issue), indicate the incorrectness to the originator.
3. If he discovers the report to have been a willful and knowing false report, convene an Ethics Hearing on the originator (not for the fact of filing, only for the willful and knowing false report).
4. Order the ethics report to remain on file.
5. Take up all the receiver's ethics reports and hold the hearing accordingly.

No person may be penalized for issuing an ethics report.

SUMMARY

IT IS A FAILURE OF THE INDIVIDUAL GROUP MEMBERS TO CONTROL THEIR FELLOWS THAT MAKES A GROUP HARD FOR ALL TO LIVE AND WORK WITH.

Only by writing Ethics Reports can bad spots in the company be recognized and corrected. For reports other than one's own will collect and point out bad conditions before they can harm the organization. This makes it a pretty rough group for a loafer or criminal to be around.

If the stats of a group, large or small, are down, try it. And get a REAL group in return that, collectively, can control the environment and prosper because its group members individually help control each other.

Successful Performance

Chapter 24

DUTIES OF AN EMPLOYEE

1. Each employee is responsible for seeing that company policy is carried out. If you see another employee at variance with company policy, it is your duty to advise him directly — if that fails, advise the Ethics Officer or the office manager.

2. Abide by the working hours of the company — arrive on time, keep a set lunch hour. If you need to change your lunch hour, check with your department head for okay. A job position not covered introduces randomity[1] into the organization.

3. Keep your own desk, equipment and work space neat and orderly. See that papers are not scattered on your desk and in your office.

4. If you see a door open with nobody on the job, close or lock the door.

5. All employees are responsible for seeing that their doors are closed or locked in the evenings; lights, radios, computers, air conditioning, etc., turned off. Leave your office clean and neat.

6. See that your supplies are adequate — order before you run out.

7. Make your daily pickups to and from the Comm Center.

8. If you change your residence or telephone number, report this information to Personnel, your department head and Reception.

9. Know the organizing board well. Know the various job positions and who covers them.

10. Abide by the purchase order system of the company.

11. Be courteous and helpful to clientele on the premises, and anyone else who visits the company. Refer people to the correct terminal. Take responsibility to see that they get to the right terminal, even if you have to walk them to the terminal's desk.

12. Keep your attire as presentable as possible. A good presentation to the public creates a good impression upon them.

13. If you see something around the premises which needs repairing, report it to the office manager.

14. Make your job position(s) real to other employees and the public.

---

[1] **randomity:** **Random** is defined as lacking a definite plan, purpose or pattern. **"-ity"** is a suffix meaning state, character, condition or an instance of any of these. **Randomity**, then, is a condition or state wherein a definite plan, purpose or pattern is lacking. [Example: Jan failed to get her position as receptionist covered during her lunch break. In her absence, customers wandered the halls looking for someone to assist them. Tremendous **randomity** ensued, as several employees were pulled off their jobs to help direct the customers.]

15. Answer people's questions. Understand the question, answer it, make friends.

16. Attend staff meetings.

17. If you receive a memo which does not pertain to your job position, reroute it. Do not attempt to handle any and every memo coming to you which is not your hat. (1) You are introducing randomity on your own job, and (2) you are handling something which another person should know and handle.

18. If you see another person not doing his job it is your duty to advise him directly. If this fails, advise his department head. Try to be helpful to him in this regard. Don't scold him or cut him down. Help him get back on the job.

19. If the organizing board does not reflect the reality of your job title(s), report this to the office manager.

20. If you occupy more than one job position and you find that you do not have enough time to devote proper attention to another of your hats so that the job is lagging or not getting done, it is your duty to iron this out with your department head in order to remedy the situation. If it is found that one of your jobs is being neglected due to lack of time available to cover it, the department head may take this up with the office manager in order to get that particular hat being worn properly. If you have too many hats, or if the workload has increased to the point that one of your hats is not worn due to lack of time to devote to it, much randomity can occur within the company itself and with the public. If you hold positions in several departments, always consult the department head under which your job position exists.

21. You are responsible for following the communications system of the company.

22. If you have questions concerning your duties in any job position, check with your department head.

23. To the best of your ability, help your fellow employees. Employees are a team, not opponents. If you see a person not doing his job, or doing it poorly, give him a hand—give him some suggestions to look over—this works better than merely scolding or criticizing him. Maybe he really doesn't know any better. It is to *your advantage* to assist your fellow employees.

24. Each employee is responsible for the company itself, for its physical appearance—its personnel—its performance. It cannot properly perform unless each employee makes it do so.

Chapter 25

PROVIDING GOOD SERVICE

The public expects good service. By this they mean positive scheduling, accurate billing, accurate addressing, and delivery of a quality product.

Also, SPEED of service is of vital importance. The prosperity of a business is directly proportional to the speed of flow of its particles (memos, goods, messengers, customers, etc.). To prosper, service must be as close to instant as possible. Anything which stops or delays the flows of a business, or delays a customer or product, or puts a customer or product on WAIT is an enemy of that business.

Good management carefully isolates all stops on its flow lines and eradicates them to increase speed of flows. Speed of service is of comparable magnitude to quality of service, and where exaggerated ideas of quality exist, they must become secondary to speed. Only then can a business prosper.

Example: Jay is a checker at a supermarket. He works the cash-only express lane. Jay believes that the most important part of his job is to provide friendly customer service. He often spends several minutes chatting with customers, discussing the weather, inquiring about their health and even their family members. Jay also accepts customers in line who have dozens of items, despite the strict company policy limiting the number of items to ten. He even allows customers to pay with credit cards if they've forgotten their cash. All this "quality service" routinely causes the express lane to be backed up at any given moment with more than a dozen impatient customers. Jay takes more time with each customer than do any of the other checkers in the store—and they don't operate an express lane! Consequently, many customers have taken their business to other grocery stores. Since Jay started working at the supermarket, customer traffic has decreased by 15%.

SENIOR POLICY: We always deliver what we promise.

It's that simple. The senior-most policy in any organization should be: We always deliver what we promise. There should be no exceptions to the rule.

GOODWILL

Goodwill is the reputation an organization has with its publics[1] for integrity, good service, prompt bill paying, high quality delivery, friendliness, etc.

For businesses that provide a technical service (e.g., health care, consulting, graphic design, auto repair, etc.), excellent technical delivery is what generates a blaze of goodwill and PR that spreads by word of mouth like wildfire. Word of mouth comes from having numerous people out in the community who are happy and cheerful and satisfied with their service. Word of mouth is a superior form of advertising to newspaper, radio and TV ads. People tend to believe their friends. They are skeptical of advertising. "It worked for Joe, it will probably work for me" is what people think.

---

[1] **publics:** (*Public Relations term*) types of audiences.

Goodwill and PR

Customer Satisfaction

THE PUBLIC KNOWS AN ORGANIZATION BY ITS APPEARANCE

Other factors also enter in where goodwill, word of mouth and PR are concerned. The public, in dealing with the business world, has grown to expect clean, pleasant offices and smart, friendly service. There is nothing as destructive of goodwill as dirty offices, sloppy "help yourself" service and an unfriendly staff.

A part of everyone's hat is keeping a good image in people and offices. Keep your desk, equipment and supplies neat and orderly. It helps. And when you see things getting broken-down or run-down or dirty, fix them or clean them or, if you can't, make it known, loud and clear, on the right comm line.

Clean offices and common areas, professional conduct, good service and above all, a friendly staff, all go a long way to promoting goodwill. It is part of *every* employee's job to help build goodwill for the organization by doing those things that will cause the public to think well of it, and by refraining from doing those things that would result in bad PR for the organization.

Chapter 26
PROFESSIONALISM

Don't ever do anything as though you were an amateur.

Anything *you do, do it as a professional, to professional standards.*

*If you have the idea about **anything** you do that you just dabble in it, you will wind up with a dabble life. There'll be no satisfaction in it because there will be no real production you can be proud of.*

Develop the frame of mind that whatever you do, you are doing it as a professional and move up to professional standards in it.

Never let it be said of you that you lived an amateur life.

*Professionals **see** situations and they handle what they see. They are not amateur dabblers.*

*So learn this as a first lesson about life. The only successful beings in any field, including living itself, are those who **have** a professional viewpoint, **make** themselves professionals and **ARE** professionals.*

Helps take the emotion @ out of decision-making. 163

APPENDIX

Table of Conditions from Non-Existence to Power Change

26. When taking over a new position, change nothing until you are thoroughly familiar with your new zone of power.	**Power Change**
25. Write up the hat for your position.	**Power**
24. Don't disconnect.	
23. Discover for yourself what *caused* the Condition of Affluence in your immediate area and strengthen it.	
22. Consolidate all gains. Any place we have gotten a gain, we keep it. Don't let things relax or go downhill or roller coaster. Any advantage or gain we have, keep it, maintain it.	**Affluence**
21. Make every action count and don't engage in any useless actions. Every new action to contribute and be of the same kind as *did* contribute.	
20. <u>*Economize* on needless or dispersed actions that did not contribute to the present condition.</u> Economize financially by knocking off all *waste*.	
19. Every time a statistic worsens slightly, quickly find out *why* and remedy it.	
18. Every time a statistic betters, look it over carefully and find out *what* bettered it. And then do that without abandoning what you were doing before. Those are the only changes you make.	**Normal Operation**
17. Ethics are very mild. The justice factor is quite mild and quite reasonable. There are no savage actions taken particularly.	
16. Don't change anything. The way you maintain an increase is, when you are in a state of Normal Operation, you don't change anything.	
15. Stiffen discipline.	
14. Prepare to deliver.	*repeat successful actions*
13. Economize.	*- bypass other leaders under you until you're comfortable w/ how things are being handled.*
12. Change your operating basis.	**Emergency**
11. Promote.	
10. Formulate and adopt firm policy that will hereafter detect and prevent the same situation from continuing to occur.	
9. Reorganize your life so that the dangerous situation is not continually happening to you.	
8. Get in your own *personal ethics* by finding what you are doing that is out-ethics and use self-discipline to correct it and get honest and straight.	**Danger**
7. Assign yourself a Danger Condition.	*Jump juniors when needed, until you're confident its back to "normal"*
6. Handle the situation and any danger in it.	
5. Bypass habits or normal routines.	
4. Do, produce and/or present it.	
3. Discover what is <u>needed</u> or wanted. — *NOT what you ~~want~~ need from them.*	
2. Make yourself known.	
1. <u>Find a communication line.</u>	**Non-Existence**

DEVELOPED TRAFFIC
SUMMARY LIST

1. False Reports
2. Non Compliances
3. Altered Compliance
4. No Reports
5. Comm Formula Unused
6. Info Failure
7. Lack of CSW
8. Suppression on Lines
9. Cross Orders
10. Present-Time Orders Only
11. Nonexistent Targeting
12. Unreal Targets
13. Cross Targets
14. Bugged Targets
15. Hobby-Horses
16. Staledated Orders and Memos
17. Formula Evasion
18. Incorrect Conditions
19. Hat Dumping
20. Channel Skips
21. Violated Purpose
22. Backlogging
23. Off-Origin (Statements and Memos)
24. Off-Line
25. Incorrect Organization
26. Organizing Board Dev-T
27. Untrained Staff
28. Unproductive Personnel
29. People Who Present Problems
30. Having to Have Before They Can Do
31. Permitting Dev-T
32. Lack of Executive Responsibility
33. Executive Enturbulence
34. Using Dev-T as an Excuse to Cut Lines
35. Catastrophes
36. Accepting an Almost
37. Failure to Get an Order Clarified
38. Irrelevant Information
39. Reasonableness
40. Failure to Handle Situations to Conclusion; Referral
41. Failure to Complete a Cycle of Action, and Referral
42. Failure to Record an Order
43. Unclear Orders
44. Misunderstood Orders
45. Relaying an Order in a Confusing Manner
46. Cleaning Cleans
47. Repeated Traffic
48. Failure to Wear Your Hat
49. Unusual Solutions
50. Removing Particles Off The Line
51. Slow Comm Lines

GLOSSARY

aberrative: (*adj.*) marked by deviation from the proper or expected course of action. [Example: *Dave's doctor warned him that exceeding the recommended dosage of the medicine would lead to **aberrative** consequences, such as headaches and nausea.*]

achieve: to get or attain by effort; gain; obtain. [Examples: *to **achieve** a solution, to **achieve** victory.*]

aftermarket: the market for replacement parts, accessories and equipment for the care or enhancement of the original product, especially an automobile, after its sale to the consumer. [Example: *The company holds a large share in the automotive radio **aftermarket**.*]

appetite over tin cup: (*American slang*) a pioneer Western U.S. term used by riverboat men on the Missouri. It means thrown away violently, like *"head over heels"* (tumbling as if in a somersault), *"bowled over"* (astonished and confused).

arbitraries: false orders or data entered into a situation or group. They exist or come about seemingly at random or by chance or as an impulsive and unreasonable act of will.

backflash: an unnecessary response to an order. It is not an acknowledgment; it is a comment or refutal.

ball-up: *noun (slang)* utter confusion; a jumbling.

beanstalk: Beanstalk is a trade name of Beanstalk Shelving Limited. **Beanstalks** are wire baskets used in communication systems in organizations. They may be attached one on top of another resulting in a system of baskets that look like a **beanstalk**.

beingness: the condition of being; the result of having assumed an identity. It could be said to be "the role in a game." In the playing of a game, each player has his own **beingness**. One's own name, one's profession, one's physical characteristics — each or all of these things could be called one's **beingness**. [Example: *Jerry was so obsessed with his **beingness** as "The CEO", that he was oblivious to the fact that not one of his staff agreed with or even responded to his communication about his mission statement.*]

blow (one's) top: (*idiom*) **1.** fly into a rage; lose one's composure. **Top** refers to the top of an erupting volcano. [Example: *If she calls about this one more time, I'm going to **blow my top**.*] **2.** go crazy, become insane.

bug: a defect or difficulty.

bugged: (*slang*) **1.** snarled up or halted. **2.** stalled. **3.** defective.

by channels: see **command channel**

camouflaged hole: Camouflage means "disguised" or made to appear as something else. When a hat is not worn for any reason at all in an organization, one gets a breakdown, a **camouflaged hole**, at that point. Somebody has a title but doesn't do the duties or actions that go with it. It looks like there is something there, but it is actually a **hole**.

campaign: a series of military operations undertaken to achieve a large-scale objective during a war. [Example: *Grant's Vicksburg **campaign** secured the entire Mississippi for the Union.*]

CC: [**C**arbon **C**opy] the field in an e-mail header that names additional recipients for the message.

channel: the proper or official course of transmission of communications. Often used in the plural: *She took her request through official **channels**.*

checkout: (*noun*) the action of verifying a person's knowledge of something, particularly an item given on a checksheet. [Example: *The training officer ordered a **checkout** of the materials John studied today.*]

checksheet: a list of materials, often divided into sections, that give the theory and practical steps which, when completed, give one a study completion. The items are selected to add up to the required knowledge of the subject.

color: character or nature. Often used in the plural. [Example: *revealed their true **colors***]

Comm Center: see **Communication Center**

Comm Formula: see **Communication Formula**

comm line: see **communication line**

command channel: a type of communication routing. **Command channels** go up through seniors, over to a senior and down to a junior. Or they go up through all seniors. It is used upward for unusual permission, authorizations, information, important actions or compliances. Downward it is used for orders. An Ethics Report routed **"by channels"** means that it is sent by the originator up through his seniors, over to the senior of the person named in the report and down to the recipient.

FLOW CHART SHOWING A REPORT BEING SENT **"BY CHANNELS"**

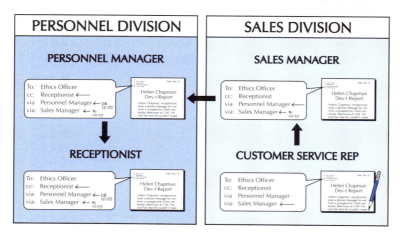

command line: a line on which authority flows (one on which orders and directives travel from senior to junior and on which compliances travel from junior to senior). In context of the org board, a **command line** is vertical.

Communication Center: The Communication Center contains a basket for each employee. Each basket is tagged with the person's name and underneath the name is his or her job title or titles. *Abbr.* **Comm Center**.

Communication Formula: The Formula of Communication is: Cause, Distance, Effect, with Intention, Attention and Duplication with Understanding. *CAUSE* is simply the source-point of emanation of the communication. *EFFECT* is the receipt-point of the communication. The communication goes across a *DISTANCE* from *CAUSE* to *EFFECT*. Both *CAUSE* and *EFFECT* must have *INTENTION* and give *ATTENTION*. For a true communication to take place, a *DUPLICATION* with *UNDERSTANDING* of what emanated from *CAUSE* must take place at *EFFECT*. *Abbr.* **Comm Formula.**

communication line: the route along which a communication (particle, message, etc.) travels from one person to another. This does not refer to physical equipment (such as a telephone line or Internet cable) but to the passage of ideas between two points. It is the line on which flow memos, voice originations and replies, information, requests, e-mails, etc. In context of the org board, a **communication line** is horizontal. *Abbr.* **comm line**.

company: a group of individuals, such as an association, corporation or partnership, associated for the purpose of carrying out, maintaining or performing a commercial or industrial enterprise.

cope: to handle any old way whatever comes up, to handle it successfully and somehow.

counter-effort: a determined attempt to do something in opposition to someone or some thing. [*Example: Refusing to keep track of his statistics on a daily basis was Josh's **counter-effort** to his senior's requirement to keep a daily graph of his production.*]

counter-intention: a determination to follow a goal which is in direct conflict with that known to be the goal(s) of the group. [*Example: Sam's determination that his company remain small and "manageable" is **counter-intention** to its goal of rapid expansion.*]

crisp: distinct and clear, without ambiguity or distortion.

crosscurrents: actions counter to the main group activity.

cross-flows: actions that flow in a contrary direction.

CSW: [**C**ompleted **S**taff **W**ork] an assembled package of information on any given situation, plan or emergency, forwarded to a senior sufficiently complete to require from that senior only an "Approved" or "Disapproved".

cycle of action: the *start-change-stop* of one's activities, body or his environment. [*Example: The sales division of a pottery manufacturing plant sold 500 flowerpots to a nursery. The plant manager, who is responsible for supervising the **cycle of action**, instructed (1) the purchaser to buy sufficient clay* (**start**), *(2) the craftsmen to make the flowerpots* (**change**) *and (3) the shipping department to deliver the items to the nursery* (**stop**).]

date coincidence: When statistics change radically for better or for worse, look for the last major alteration or broad general action that occurred just before it and it is usually the reason for the change. In other words, a specific major change in what one normally did or does could result in a dramatically changed statistic. All one need do is ask, "What changed?" when looking at a radical increase or decrease in a statistic, and he will find the occurrence that coincided with the changed statistic and the date that it happened. We call this the **date coincidence**. Once spotted, one can then take the appropriate action to reverse the decline or reinforce the increase in the statistic.

deep-six: (*idiom*) a discarding or disposing of something. To *"end up with a **deep-six**"* means to *end up being discarded or disposed of*. [This is a nautical expression indicating a water depth of 6 fathoms (36 feet); **deep-six** acquired its idiomatic definition from the fact that something thrown overboard at or greater than this depth would be difficult, if not impossible, to recover.]

delirium tremens: (*Latin*) also called **the d.t.'s**, a withdrawal syndrome occurring in persons who have developed physiological dependence on alcohol. It is characterized by trembling, sweating, acute anxiety, confusion and hallucinations.

department: a portion of a division in an organization, headed by an executive, which is responsible for the performance of certain functions or production of certain products. [Examples: *the Purchasing **Department**, the Printing **Department***]

dev-t: [**dev**eloped **t**raffic] unusual and unnecessary traffic.

division: a part of an organization. [Examples: *the research **division** of a company; the engineering **division** of a university*]

dodge: (*noun*) an expedient; something contrived or used to meet an urgent need. [Example: *During the annual product inventory, rather than counting each item in accordance with company policy, Joe would use his favorite **dodge** of counting stacks of products, making the assumption that each stack contained 50 units.*]

downstat: one who has low or declining personal production statistics. A **downstat** group would be a group whose overall production statistics are low or declining.

duties: any actions, tasks, etc., required by or relating to one's occupation or position. [Example: *the **duties** of a secretary*]

dwindling spiral: The worse an individual or situation gets, the more capacity he or it has to get worse. ***Spiral*** refers to a progressive downward movement, marking a relentlessly deteriorating state of affairs, and considered to take the form of a **spiral**. The term comes from aviation, where it is used to describe the phenomenon of a plane descending and spiraling in smaller and smaller circles, as in an accident or feat of expert flying, which, if not handled, can result in loss of control and a crash.

dynamics: There could be said to be eight urges (drives, impulses) in life. These are called ***dynamics***. They are the central drives of an individual. Every individual is possessed of an urge for survival on every one of the eight **dynamics**. The ***First Dynamic*** is the urge toward survival as one's self. Here we have individuality expressed fully. The

Second Dynamic is the urge toward survival through (a) procreation and (b) the family unit, including the rearing of children. It would concern itself with the affinity for and communication with a mate or children. The *Third Dynamic* is the urge toward survival through the group and as the group. Any group (social and political as well as commercial) could be considered to be a part of the Third **Dynamic**. The school, the business, the society, the town and the nation are each *part* of the Third **Dynamic** and each one *is* a Third **Dynamic**. The *Fourth Dynamic* is the urge toward survival through Mankind as a whole. Whereas one race would be considered a Third **Dynamic**, all the races would be considered the Fourth **Dynamic**. The *Fifth Dynamic* is the urge toward survival through life forms. This includes all living things, whether plant or animal, that are directly and intimately motivated by *life*. The *Sixth Dynamic* is the urge toward survival through the physical universe and has as its components Matter, Energy, Space and Time. The *Seventh Dynamic* is the urge toward survival as a spiritual being. Anything spiritual (e.g., ESP, intuition) would come under this heading. The *Eighth Dynamic* is the urge toward survival through the Supreme Being or, more exactly, Infinity. It will be found amongst individuals that each person stresses one of the **dynamics** more than the others, or may stress a combination of **dynamics** as more important than other combinations. No one of these **dynamics**, from one to seven, is more important than any other one of them in terms of orienting the individual. The abilities and shortcomings of individuals can be understood by viewing their participation in the various **dynamics**. For example, a person who is incapable of operating on the Third **Dynamic** is incapable at once of being a part of a team and so might be said to be incapable of a social existence.

echelon: one of a series of levels or grades in an organization or field of activity.

embroidered: embellished with fictitious additions or exaggerations.

engagement: a hostile encounter; a battle.

entheta: [*en-*, enturbulated + *theta*, thought or life. *Enturbulated:* caused to be turbulent or agitated and disturbed. *Theta*, the eighth letter of the Greek alphabet, means *thought* or *life* or *the spirit*.] **Entheta** means irrational or confused or destructive thought. It especially refers to communications, which, based on lies and confusions, are slanderous, choppy or destructive. **Entheta** can also consist of anger, sarcasm, despair or slyly destructive suggestions.

ethics: 1. the rules or standards governing the conduct of a person (*personal* **ethics**) or the conduct of the members of a profession (e.g., *business* **ethics** or *medical* **ethics**). **Ethics** actually consists of rationality toward the highest level of survival for the individual, the group, mankind and the other dynamics taken up collectively. **Ethics** are reason. **Ethics** are the actions an individual takes on himself in order to accomplish optimum survival for himself and others on all dynamics. It is a personal thing. It is a First Dynamic action. 2. (*capitalized*) **Ethics:** the Ethics Section of an organization.

ethics actions: any disciplinary measures taken with an employee to address and remove demonstrated counter-intentions from the environment. *Counter-intention* means a determination to follow a goal which is in direct conflict with that known to be the goal(s) of the group.

fireman: the person who tends the fire of a steam engine; a stoker.

flap: something (as an incident or remark) that generates an uproar.

flubs: embarrassing, clumsy mistakes.

foment: (*noun*) state of excitation.

form of the organization: the lines, actions, spaces and flows of an organization, worked out and controlled by employees who are specialists in their respective job functions. These specialists are grouped in departments which have certain actions in common. The departments, having similar functions, are grouped into divisions. The divisions combine into the whole org form. To **hold the form of the org** means seniors ordering the right orders to the right specialists and targeting their production.

formula: in general, a prescribed form or rule; a fixed or conventional method in which anything is to be done, arranged or said.

get away with murder: (*figurative expression*) to commit an act for which one could incur strong disapproval or harsh criticism without being punished.

glib: marked by disassociation of oneself from the materials one is studying. One doesn't associate the materials with anything; the words enter into one's consciousness on the surface only, with no awareness of the concepts they represent. The **glib student** can repeat what he's read or heard, but can't apply.—**glibly** (*adverb*) in a **glib** manner, —**glibness** (*noun*) the state of being **glib**.

going concern: a business or job position that is operating successfully and is likely to continue to do so.

graph: a line or diagram showing how one quantity depends on, compares with or changes another. It is any pictorial device used to display numerical relationships.

grasp: to take hold of mentally; understand; comprehend.

grooved in: shown how something works so one can then operate it or handle it. Usually, a *groove-in* is a short action covering the basics of how something works or functions and is thus different from an apprenticeship, which is a longer, more detailed action.

hat: **1.** a term used to describe the write-ups, checksheets and packs that outline the purposes, know-how and duties of a job position. [Example: *Upon arrival at the office, John's boss gave him a binder containing the **hat** for his new job, with instructions to read it within a week.*] **2.** slang for the title and work of a job position in an organization. Taken from the fact that in many professions such as railroading, the type of hat worn is the badge of the job. [Example: *Mary wears two **hats** in her company, that of receptionist and mailroom clerk.*] **3.** (*verb*) to instruct a person in the proper performance of one or more aspects of his job. [Example: *The first action Dave took to improve his department's customer service feedback score was to **hat** his juniors on proper phone etiquette.*]

hatted: fully trained to do the specific functions of one's job.

havingness: the feeling that one owns or possesses. In an organization, one's **havingness** could be achieved or increased by such things as a pay raise, new health benefits, a bonus, earned rewards, recognition or stock in the company.

hobby-horse: one's favorite topic, idea or project. To **ride a hobby-horse** means to order and comply only in one's favorite area, neglecting areas of greater importance.

inspection before the fact: inspection before anything bad has happened.

jam(med): (*verb*) to block, congest or clog. [Example: *a drain that was jammed by debris*]

Job Endangerment Report: an Ethics Report that one files on his next highest superior in the event that he is given orders or directions or preventions or denied materials which make it hard or impossible for him to raise his statistics or do his job at all. While a **Job Endangerment Report** may be filed on anyone (superiors, equals or juniors), it is normally filed on a direct senior who has issued an order that endangered one's job by demanding one alter or depart from known policy.

jockey: to direct or maneuver (something) by skill for one's advantage.

junior: an immediate subordinate employee; also referred to as a *direct report* in some companies. [Example: *John scheduled meetings with each of his **juniors** to evaluate their job performances.*]

justice: the action taken on the individual by the group when he fails to get his own ethics in, i.e., when he fails to take the actions that would accomplish optimum survival for himself and others. **Justice** means fair and equitable treatment for both the group and the individual.

know-how: knowledge of how to do something smoothly and efficiently; technical expertise, practical knowledge.

line(s): A **line** is a route along which a particle travels between one terminal and the next in an organization; it is a fixed pattern of terminals who originate and receive, or receive and relay, orders, information or other particles.

management: **1.** the planning of means to attain determined goals, assigning them to staff for execution, and proper coordination of activities within the group to attain maximum efficiency with minimal effort. **2.** the person or persons controlling or directing the affairs of a business, institution, organization, etc. [Example: *The store is under new **management**.*]

materiel: all the apparatus, equipment, parts and supplies (as distinguished from the personnel) required in an operation, organization or undertaking.

memo: see **memorandum**

memorandum: a communication, usually brief, written for interoffice circulation. It may contain directive, advisory or informative matter. *Abbr.* **memo**.

morals: a code of good conduct laid down out of the experience of a culture or society to serve as a uniform yardstick for the conduct of individuals and groups. **Morals** are actually laws.

mores: (pronounced ***mor·aze***) the customs and manners of a social group or culture. **Mores** often serve as moral guidelines for acceptable behavior but are not necessarily religious or ethical.

off-line: A **line** is a route along which a particle travels between one terminal and the next in an organization; it is a fixed pattern of terminals who originate and receive, or receive and relay, orders, information or other particles. A person is *on-line* when he uses the pattern of the organization correctly. If he does not, he is **off-line**. [Example: *Joe personally delivers a memo to Bill. Joe is **off-line** because he didn't use the Comm Center, which is the correct line for written communication.* Example: *Mary needs a new desk. She goes to the Personnel Director to order the desk. However, it is not Personnel's job to order office furniture. Mary presented herself to the wrong terminal; she is **off-line**.*] A particle, such as a memo, is **off-line** when it is sent to the wrong person.

off-origin: a term designating things *originated* by a terminal that do not apply to or aren't the business of his job position; a type of dev-t where a terminal originates something not his hat. [Example: *an **off-origin** memo would be a memo originated by someone that should have been originated by someone else.*]

on record: (*idiom*) existing as a matter of public knowledge; known.

order: a direction or command issued by an authorized person to a person or group (section, department, etc.) within the sphere of the authorized person's authority. By implication, an **order** goes from a senior to juniors.

org board: see **organizing board**

organization: **1.** the act of arranging personnel and materials in an orderly or systematic way. **Organization** consists of certain people doing certain jobs. The purpose of **organization** is to make planning become actuality. **2.** a number of persons or groups having specific responsibilities and united for some purpose or work; a company.

organize: 1. to arrange in an orderly or systematic way. **2.** to set up an administrative structure for.

organizing board: a board which displays the functions, duties, sequences of action and authorities of an organization. The **organizing board** shows the pattern of organizing to obtain a product. The result of the whole **organizing board** is a product. The product of each hat on the board adds up to the total product of the organization. *Abbr.* **org board**.

out-ethics: 1. an action or situation in which an individual is involved that is contrary to the ideals and best interests of his group. **2.** an act or situation or relationship that is contrary to the ethics standards, codes or ideals of the group or other members of the group. **3.** an act of omission or commission by an individual that could or has reduced the general effectiveness of a group or its other members. **4.** an individual act of omission or commission which impedes the general well-being of a group or impedes it in achieving its goals.

outness: a deviation from what is accurate or right; something in disagreement or at variance with the correct procedures or optimum conditions in an organization. [Example: *Not* *using the proper procedure to route incoming phone calls, resulting in calls being lost, is an **outness**.*] To be a good executive or employee, one has to know the right way something is done and to be able to apply and get done what he knows and be able to correct **outnesses** so they go back to the correct procedures.

overwhelm: (*noun*) a state wherein one is overcome or overpowered in mind or feeling, so great as to make opposition (to a force, idea, concept, etc.) useless. [Example: *Dorothy realizes she has absolutely no control over the weather, and that she can't predict or prevent tornadoes, no matter how much she learns about them or how much responsibility she tries to take. Consequently, during tornado season, she ends up in an **overwhelm**.*]

pack: a collection of written materials which match a checksheet. A **pack** does not necessarily include a booklet or hardcover book that may be called for as part of a checksheet.

particle: a generic term used to describe any item being processed or handled in an organization, whether it be a person (e.g., a customer), a phone message, a memo, raw materials, etc.

pet hate: (*idiom*) *British English*, also **pet peeve** *American English*, something that is disliked intensely and is a constant or repeated annoyance.

physical universe: a **universe** is the sphere or realm in which something exists or takes place. The **physical universe** is the universe of the planets, their rocks, rivers and oceans, etc. It is composed of Matter, Energy, Space and Time.

pitch: the degree of inclination or slope; angle.

police: to control, regulate or keep in order. One **polices** dev-t by watching for dev-t, spotting it and rapidly getting it off his lines.

policies: the rules and administrative formulas by which members of an organization agree on action and conduct their affairs.

position: the name of the particular job one holds in any business which has its own distinguishing duties, responsibilities and products in relation to the other jobs in that business.

posting: placing a person in an assigned area of responsibility and action, which is supervised in part by an executive.

PRing: PR [**P**ublic **R**elations] is *good works well publicized*. It consists of those functions of a corporation, organization, etc., concerned with attempting to create favorable public opinion for itself. **PR** can be corrupted to "a technique of lying convincingly." Used as a slang expression, **PRing** means putting up a lot of false reports to serve as a smoke screen for idleness or bad actions. [Example: *John was having quite a lot of trouble making his sales quota. He was merely **PRing** his boss when he said that he expected to have his best month ever.*]

product: a finished, high-quality service or article in the hands of the consumer as an exchange for a valuable.

program: a series of steps in sequence to carry out a plan. **Programs** are written at division level or above and are made up of all types of targets coordinated and executed on time. **Programs** written and executed at departmental level in a company are called **mini programs**.

project: a series of guiding steps written in sequence to carry out one step of a program, which, if followed, will result in a full and successful accomplishment of the program target.

publics: (*Public Relations term*) types of audiences.

purpose: the entire concept of an ideal scene for any activity. [Example: *Lisa's organizational **purpose** as the receptionist is to receive particles of all types and route them expeditiously to the appropriate terminals, according to the organizing board.*]

quota: a production assignment. It would be the number assigned to whatever is produced.

randomity: Random is defined as lacking a definite plan, purpose or pattern. **"-ity"** is a suffix meaning state, character, condition or an instance of any of these. **Randomity**, then, is a condition or state wherein a definite plan, purpose or pattern is lacking. [Example: *Jan failed to get her position as receptionist covered during her lunch break. In her absence, customers wandered the halls looking for someone to assist them. Tremendous **randomity** ensued, as several employees were pulled off their jobs to help direct the customers.*]

rat's nest: (*informal*) a place of great clutter or disorder.

read: to examine and grasp the meaning of a graphic representation.

reasonable: accepting or tolerant of faulty explanations. Being **reasonable** is a symptom of being unable to recognize illogical data for what they are and being unable to use the data to discover actual situations.

roller coaster: (*verb*) to move steeply up and down; to rise and fall like a **roller coaster** ride.

rote: 1. (*noun*) a memorizing process using routine or repetition, often without full attention or comprehension. **2.** (*adj.*) learned or memorized **by rote**. **3.** (*idiom*) **by rote**: from memory, without thought of the meaning; in a mechanical way. [Example: *to learn a language **by rote**]

section: a portion of a department.

senior: one's immediate superior in the workplace, i.e., the person to whom one reports directly in an organization; supervisor. [Example: *My **senior** gave me the day off.*]

service facilities: Facilities are things that make an action, operation or course of conduct easier. When a senior executive has the ability to make money for the organization or greatly raise statistics, and when this ability has been demonstrated, that executive should have **facilities**. They normally include those things that unburden lines, speed lines, gather data, compile, buy leisure, defend, and extend longevity on the job. A **service facility** is simply a person, such as an assistant, or an item of equipment that facilitates an executive's ability to provide more, better or faster service.

spring fever: the laziness or restlessness that many people feel during the first warm, sunny days of spring.

stable terminal: a person to whom programs, projects and orders may be given with the sure knowledge that they will be complied with and executed.

staledating, -ated: The term **staledate** means any memo or answer to a memo that is older in date than one should reasonably expect when he receives it. **Staledating** is the act of causing a written communication or the response to a communication to become a **staledate**. In such instances, the memo or answer to the memo is said to be **staledated**.

standing order: an instruction or prescribed procedure in force permanently or until changed or canceled.

statistic(s): a number or amount *compared* to an earlier number or amount of the same thing. **Statistics** refer to the quantity of work done or the value of it in money. *Abbr.* **stat(s)**.

string a line: (*idiom*) to establish a fixed pattern of terminals who originate and receive, or receive and relay, orders, information or other particles. [Example: *For his new brochure project, the marketing director* **strung a line** *between the account rep and the graphic design artist so that client input regarding content would be taken into account when designing the brochure.*]

study: (*noun*) the pursuit of a particular branch of learning, science or art. [Example: *the* **study** *of law*]

sundering: breaking or wrenching apart; severing.

target(s): an objective one intends to accomplish within a given period of time.

targeting: establishing what action or actions should be undertaken in order to achieve a desired objective.

technology: 1. the methods of application of an art or science as opposed to mere knowledge of the science or art itself. **2.** the whole body of the science. *Abbr.* **tech**.

terminal: a point that receives, relays and sends communication or other particles in a company. A person located at such a point is commonly referred to as a **terminal**.

Third World countries: The term **"Third World"** refers to those countries, mostly former colonies that maintained their independence, that were not politically aligned with the West (the industrialized capitalist world, the "First World") or with the former Soviet Union and its allies (the "Second World"). However, the term can be misleading and, consequently, it has outlived its usefulness. It suggests a uniformity among countries that are extremely varied economically as well as culturally, socially and politically. They all share an objection to colonization and to foreign domination generally, but they hardly constitute a cohesive political force. The only characteristic common in all **Third World countries** is that their governments demand and receive Western aid. Today, the countries of the **Third World** are more commonly referred to as "developing countries". A developing country is a country that has low standards of democratic governments, industrialization, social programs and human rights guarantees that are yet to develop to those standards met in the West.

top management: the highest ranking executives (with titles such as Chief Executive Officer, President, Vice President, Executive Director, etc.) responsible for the entire organization. **Top management** lays down and/or okays policy, programs and plans.

traffic: communication, dealings or contact between persons or groups.

trend: an inclination toward a general course or direction.

unbugged: (*slang*) unsnarled or gotten moving again.

upper echelon: the higher level of any group. In business organizations, this refers to senior executives. [Example: *Mark's new customer service campaign involved employees at every level, including the **upper echelon**.*]

upstat: one who has high personal production statistics. An **upstat** group would be a group whose overall production statistics are high.

viability: the longevity, usefulness and desirability of the product. **Viability** depends, in the main, upon exchange where economics are concerned.

waffle: 1. to pause or hold back in uncertainty or unwillingness. **2.** to be unable to make a decision; vacillate.

wilco: (*interjection*) [**wil**l **co**mply] an expression used especially in radio communications to indicate agreement or compliance.

wreak havoc: to bring about or cause disorder or chaos.

write-up: a written description of the operating procedures of a job position. This often includes a summary of the job functions, which is usually provided by the person who previously held the position.

INDEX

A

accepting an almost, 133

acknowledgment,
definition, 32
what an executive wants on his lines, 32

Action Affluence Formula, 58

affinity,
and reality are very much less important than communication, 6
and the ARC Triangle, 6
component of Understanding, 1
definition, 1

Affluence,
Action Affluence Formula, 58
Condition of –, 57
description of slant of line on graph, 71
Formula, 58
most touchy Condition there is, 57
Power and –, 59

Affluence Attainment, 63

Affluence Formula, see **Affluence**

agreement,
is an element of coordination, 101
reality is –, 1

altered compliance, 117

approval,
completed staff work and –, 111
how to get approval of actions and projects, 111
is usually worked for far harder than mere pay, 149
lack of CSW slows down –, 119

ARC (Affinity, Reality, Communication)
good coordination of team effort results in high –, 101
is the common denominator to all of life's activities, 6
not an equilateral triangle, 6
restoring –, 7
Triangle, 6

ARC break(s)
definition, 7
you can develop more traffic internally, more upsets and more *ARC breaks* than anything you can mention (Dev-T #40), 135

B

backflashes, 29

backlog(s)(ing), 127

battle plan(s),
definition, 97
production and –, 99
staff meeting and –, 102
versus *strategy*, 97
weekly Conditions formulas and –, 99

beanstalk, 108

be, do and have,
and subproduct lists, 42

busy(ness),
dev-t and traffic –, 115
making a staff – (with busywork), 43
no need to look busy if you are not –, 141

by channels, see **command channel**

bypass(ing), see also **Danger**
Danger Formula and –, 54
definition, 54
First Dynamic Danger Formula and –, 55

C

camouflaged hole, 115, 139

channel,
by –s, 152
command –, 152
definition, 126
– Skips (Dev-T #20), 126

clean,
cleaning –s, (Dev-t #46), 138
leave your office clean and neat, 157
offices go a long way to promoting goodwill, 160
public has grown to expect clean, pleasant offices, 160

command channel,
definition, 152

command line,
definition, 25
is vertical, 25

Comm Center, *see* **Communication Center**

communication,
affinity and reality are very much less important than –, 6
and the ARC Triangle, 6
component of Understanding, 3
definition, 3
memorandum, or *memo*, is a –, 105
music is a very fine means of –, 3
obsessive or compulsive, 5
that *can* be put in writing *should* be put in writing, 26
two kinds of –, 3

Communication Center,
as the org board is changed, the Comm Center baskets are changed, 108
daily pickups to and from the –, 157
description, 107
every employee has a basket in the –, 108

Communication Formula, 4

communication line(s),
definition, 25
finding a –, 52
is horizontal, 25
jamming a –, 26-28
it's a serious thing to jam an executive's –, 29
putting erroneous data on the –, 28
Slow (Dev-t #51) –, 140
to string a –, 29
what an executive wants on his incoming –, 32

Completed Staff Work,
correct example, 113
CSWP, meaning of, 114
definition, 111
description, 112
incomplete staff work, effect of, 111-112
is an assembled memo or packet, 112
is what executives want, 114
junior must state or initial "This is okay" on all work, actions or projects, 106, 114, 131
lack of –, 119
requiring only an "approved" or "not approved", 111

sample format, 114
wrong example, 112

compliance,
accepting an almost –, 133
altered –, 117

Condition(s),
Action Affluence Formula, 58
Affluence Attainment, 62, 63
Affluence Formula, 58
assigned to statistic trends, 76
below Non-Existence, 65
completing formulas, 73
correct designation of –, 61
Danger Formula, 54
definition, 51
Doubt Formula, 66
Emergency Formula, 56
example of completed Danger Formula, 89-90
example of completed Doubt Formula, 67-68
Expanded Non-Existence Formula, 53
First Dynamic Danger Formula, 55
Formula Evasion (Dev-t #17), 125
formulas flow one to the next, 73
from Non-Existence through Power are declared on the basis of statistics, 51
in weekly assignments one only considers two things, 69
Incorrect Conditions (Dev-t #18), 126
Liability Formula, 66
Non-Existence Formula, 52
Normal Formula, 57
Power Change Formula, 60
Power Formula, 59
Scale of –, 51
there is no rote method of determining the Condition of a stat, 74
topic covered in a staff meeting, 102

control,
and the K-R-C Triangle, 10
definition, 9
examples of a group member not exerting –, 152
is summed up in the ability to *start*, *change* and *stop*, 10
person who is hatted can control his job position, 9

coordination,
elements of –, 101
is the essence of management, 101

cope,
and organize, 22
how to move out of –, 23
remaining in –, 22

counter-effort(s), 147

counter-intention(s), 147

courage, 11

CSW, see **Completed Staff Work**

cycle of action,
and org board, 21
failure to complete a –, 136
targeting –, 89

D

Danger,
Condition, 54
Condition is normally assigned when, 54
description of slant of line on graph, 70
First Dynamic Danger Formula, 55
Formula, 54

Danger Formula, see **Danger**

decision(s),
demands for –, 29
depending on execs for petty –, 29

department(s)(al),
and duties of an employee, 157-158
and the principles of exchange, 41
and Violated Purpose (Dev-T #21), 127
Communications Dept. manager, 108
every department should have an assigned statistic, 87
middle management, 98
minor hirings and firings in a –, 32
one can always judge the state of a department by the state of its comm baskets, 109
reads its statistics by the *day*, 69
stats at staff meetings, 102
there should always be some individual assigned as responsible for the work or production of every –, 87
whole theory of successful organization is to have departments that specialize, 17

dispatch, 105

developed traffic,
Accepting An Almost, 133
Altered Compliance, 117
and CSW's, 111
Backlogging, 127
Bugged Targets, 123
Catastrophes, 133
Channel Skips, 126
Cleaning Cleans, 138
Comm Formula Unused, 118
costs a company the services of two thirds of its personnel, 115
Cross Orders, 120
Cross Targets, 123
definition, 115
Executive Enturbulence, 132
Failure To Complete A Cycle Of Action, and Referral, 136
Failure To Get An Order Clarified, 134
Failure To Handle Situations To Conclusion; Referral, 135
Failure To Record An Order, 136
Failure To Wear Your Hat, 139
False Reports, 116
Formula Evasion, 125
Hat Dumping, 126
Having To Have Before They Can Do, 130
Hobby-Horses, 124
Incorrect Conditions, 126
Incorrect Organization, 128
Info Failure, 119
Irrelevant Information, 134
Lack of CSW, 119
Lack of Executive Responsibility, 131
Misunderstood Orders, 137
No Reports, 117
Non Compliances, 116
Nonexistent Targeting, 122
Off-Line, 128
Off-Origin, 127
Organizing Board Dev-T, 129
People Who Present Problems, 130
Permitting Dev-T, 130-131
Present-Time Orders Only, 121
Reasonableness, 135
Relaying An Order In A Confusing Manner, 138
Removing Particles Off The Line, 140
Repeated Traffic, 138
Slow Comm Lines, 140
Staledated Orders and Memos, 125
Suppression on Lines, 120
Unclear Orders, 137
Unproductive Personnel, 130
Unreal Targets, 122-123
Untrained Staff, 129
Unusual Solutions, 139
Using Dev-T As An Excuse To Cut Lines, 132
Violated Purpose, 127

dev-t log, 132, 152

division(s)(al),
    and strategy, 97
    and the principles of exchange, 41
    and Violated Purpose (Dev-T #21), 127
    Comm Centers, 108
    every division should have an assigned statistic, 87
    Human Resources –, 147
    middle management, 98
    one reads the division statistics for the *week* in an organization, 69
    stats at staff meetings, 102
    targets and quotas, 88
    there should always be some individual assigned as responsible for the work or production of every –, 87
    whole theory of successful organization is to have divisions that specialize, 17

Doubt,
    Condition, 66
    example of a completed formula, 67-68
    Formula, 66

Doubt Formula, *see* **Doubt**

down-statistic(s), *see* **statistics**

duty(ies),
    of an employee (list), 157-158
    of an employee *to round up the comm lines that relate to his job position*, 53
    of the Inspections Officer, 147
    to advise another employee at variance with company policy, 157
    to advise another employee who is not doing his job, 158

dwindling spiral, 7, 8

dynamics,
    ethics and –, 63, 146
    decide on the basis of the greatest number of dynamics (Doubt Formula), 66
    increasing KRC on all –, 10, 11
    out-ethics and –, 146

E

efficiency,
    and Power Condition, 59
    by writing CSW's, you increase office –, 114
    valid subproduct list will greatly increase organization –, 43

embroidered reports, 31

Emergency,
    Condition, 55
    Danger Condition assigned when it has continued too long, 54
    description of slant of line on graph, 70
    Formula, 56
    Formula applied to unsuccessful replacements, 61
    unchanging statistic is not stable, 56

Emergency Formula, *see* **Emergency**

employee(s),
    are expected to do their jobs, 149
    backflash is a disease peculiar to only a few, 29
    can be "reasonable" and accept reasons why something cannot be done, 135
    can "ride his favorite hobby-horse", ordering and complying only in his favorite area, neglecting areas of greater importance, 124
    Comm Center contains a basket for each –, 107
    create a bottleneck when they jam a line to an executive, 29
    dev-t costs a company two-thirds of the efforts of its –, 115
    duties of an – (list), 157-158
    each employee must know who is wearing the other hats in the company so he can send *their* work to them, 17
    each employee should keep a daily graph, 91
    ethics actions are often used to handle down-statistics of the individual, 150
    every employee has one or more products, 40
    exchange in abundance is the key to howling success for the individual, 47
    good org board is well grooved in with each –, 23
    has to know more jobs in the company than his own, 33
    internal demand of one to another is what really determines the condition of the group, 47
    it is the duty of any employee to *round up the communication lines that relate to his job position*, 53
    it is up to the individual employee what the company income is and what his own pay is, 47
    many employees misapply the Non-Existence Formula, 52

most common failure of any employee lies in the inability to NAME YOUR PRODUCT, 40

should be gathered together, once a week, to hold a staff meeting, 101

should be required to report weekly the statistic of every job for which he or she is responsible, 87

stats show whether an employee or group is working or not working, 69

unwilling employee always makes dev-t out of every situation, problem, order and policy, 115

who is a flagrant dev-t source, 130

entheta,
a comm line can be jammed due to –, 26
means embroidered reports, 31

enturbulence,
executive, 132

error,
inspection before the fact, 136

ethics,
actions, 147, 150
are reason, 146
are the actions an individual takes on himself in order to accomplish optimum survival for himself and others on all dynamics, 63
are very mild (Normal Formula), 57
by monitoring daily graphs, ethics can be put in where the individual appears incapable of keeping his own in, 92
definition, 63, 145-146
design of –, 145
get in your own *personal ethics* (First Dynamic Danger Formula), 55
how they differ from morals, 145
very easy for an employee to completely misunderstand – and its functions, 150
you have got to stiffen ethics (Emergency Formula), 56

Ethics,
abbreviated term for the Ethics Section, 147
a person who is not doing his job becomes the focus of investigation by Ethics, 150
only exists to hold the fort long enough... to get technology in, 148
protection, 150
violation of company policy regarding dev-t is reported in writing to Ethics, 152

Ethics Officer,
conducts investigations, 147, 154
eliminating counter-efforts, 147
primary function is to support and protect employees who are doing their jobs well, 147
primary goal is to facilitate the company's expansion and ensure its future survival, 148
removing counter-intentions, 147
runs the Ethics Section, 147

Ethics Reports,
are addressed to the Ethics Officer, 152
disputed –, 154
may be written on matters such as..., 152
only by writing Ethics Reports can bad spots in the company be recognized and corrected, 154
Sample Ethics Report, 153

exchange(d)(able),
company income and payroll, 45
Condition #1, rip-off, defined, 45
Condition #2, partial exchange, defined, 45
Condition #3, fair exchange, defined, 46
Condition #4, exchange in abundance, defined, 46
conditions of –, 45
criminal exchange defined, 45
group *internal* pressure and the conditions of –, 47
is product, 39
short-changing, 45
unless a product is exchangeable, it's not a product at all, 39
VFP is something that can be –, 41

executive(s),
applies the Danger Formula when he assigns a junior or area under his control a Condition of Danger, 54
can get his stats rising by setting quotas, 93
depended on for petty decisions is sure to jam lines and cost income, 29
Enturbulence (Dev-T #33), 132
Failure to Record an Order (Dev-T #42), 136
gives an unclear order (Dev-T #43), 137
is utterly dependent upon the willingness of those who work for him, 35
Lack of Responsibility (Dev-T #32), 131
Reasonableness (Dev-T #39), 135
role of –, 29
same traffic repeated to the same – (Dev-T #47), 138
string lines, 29

want Completed Staff Work, 114
what an – wants on his lines, 29
what an –'s lines should look like, 32

F

fact,
    inspection before the –, 136

failure,
    Info – (Dev-T #6), 119
    most common failure of any employee lies in NAME YOUR PRODUCT, 40
    of the individual group members to control their fellows, 154
    to Complete a Cycle of Action, and Referral (Dev-T #41) 136
    to comply with an order, 116
    to Get an Order Clarified (Dev-T #37), 134
    to Handle Situations to Conclusion; Referral (Dev-T #40), 135
    to Record an Order (Dev-T #42), 136
    to wear another hat that isn't yours, now and then, 33
    to Wear Your Hat (Dev-T #48), 139

fair exchange, 45, 46, 47

form of the organization, 121, 122

G

goodwill,
    and VFPs, 41
    definition, 159
    high affinity includes all feelings of –, 1
    it is part of every employee's job to help build –, 160
    PR and –, 159

graph(s)(ing),
    accumulating graph, described, 91
    Condition assignments and –, 69
    correct scale, example, 86
    correct scaling is the essence of good –, 86
    daily –, 91
    incorrect scale, example, 85
    need not figure scale for more than one graph at a time, 84
    properly scaling statistic –, 84
    quotas set with idea of creating continually rising stat –, 88
    upside down –, 72
    what to do if your stat indicates you've moved up a Condition before you even have a chance to finish a formula, 73

H

handle(ing),
    a dip in a Power statistic with the appropriate Condition formula, 74
    Affluence right, and it's a rocket ride, 57
    and control the people with whom one is surrounded is a vital part of success, v
    ethics actions are often used to handle down-statistics, 150
    everything you don't handle comes back and bites, 141
    professionals handle what they see, 161
    something not yours, 33
    the situation and any danger in it (Danger Formula), 54
    the situation and any danger in it (First Dynamic Danger Formula), 55
    the types of particles of the organization, 23
    your memos daily, 107
    work, how to –, 141

hat(s)(ted)(ting),
    beware of wearing hats other than your own, 19
    by monitoring daily graphs, hatting can occur, 92
    Completed Staff Work, the most important piece of your –, 111
    definition, ix, 17
    disorganization consists of each person wearing all hats regardless of assignment, 17
    – , DON'T HIT personnel, 147
    – Dumping (Dev-t #19), 126
    each person wears his own assigned –, 18
    failure to wear another hat that isn't yours now and then may cause more confusion than doing *only* your job, 33
    Failure To Wear Your – (Dev-t #48), 139
    part of everyone's hat is keeping a good image in people and offices, 160
    person who is hatted can control his job position, 9
    Power Formula, Step 2: Write up the hat for your job position, 59
    to get anywhere in GETTING a product, one has to spend some time hatting, 40
    wearing too many –, 158
    when one is hatted, he knows the technology of HANDLING things, 10

I

ideal scene,
    using KRC to go more toward an –, 10

idleness,
    found where statistics continue to go down, 54
    of equipment or personnel that should be in action, 152

in-basket(s),
    dev-t (Item #31) and overflowing –, 130
    divisional –, 108
    keep it empty, 109
    taking comm particles out of another's –, 140

in-charge(s),
    routing and –, 17
    separates into types or classes of thing or action, 18
    title for the head of a section, 88

income,
    depending on an executive for petty decisions is sure to jam lines and cost –, 29
    eating up an executive's time destroys –, 29
    exchange, company income & payroll, 45
    is raised by the competent use of targeting in battle plans, 99
    it is up to the individual employee what the company income is and what his own pay is, 47

information,
    element of coordination, 101
    what an executive wants on his lines, 32

inspection,
    before the fact, 136
    graph posted for, 93

Inspections Section, 147

Inspections and Reports, 147

Inspections Officer,
    basic duties of, 147
    HAT! DON'T HIT personnel, 147
    monitors the company's statistic graphs, 147
    Things That Shouldn't Be, 153

integrity,
    goodwill and –, 159

investigation,
    by Ethics, 147-148, 150

"Is this okay?", 114, 131

J

jam(s)(med)(ming),
    comm line, ways it can be –, 26-28
    depending on an executive for petty decisions is sure to jam lines, 29
    employees create a bottleneck when they jam a line to an executive, 29
    Illegal policy set at unauthorized levels jams the actions of a group, 121
    one consequence of noncompliance when repeated over a long period is to move a large number of targets into present time in a sort of frantic –, 117
    only an executive can resolve the jams that impede things, 29

job(s)
    ability to hold a job depends on ability, v
    are not held by flukes or fate or fortune, v
    assuming job positions, 61
    collapsed job position is taken over in Non-Existence, 62
    dev-t means "responsibility for your job is very low", 115
    employees *are* expected to do their –, 149
    every job should have an assigned statistic, 87
    if you see another person not doing his –, 158
    make the title and duties of your job position known to others, 34
    make your job position(s) real to other employees and the public, 157
    most common cause of unacceptable production on the –, 15
    new job is taken over in Non Existence, 61
    only a few employees are dedicated to not doing their –, 151
    organization consists of certain people doing certain –, 17
    part of *every* employee's job is to help build goodwill, 160
    person doing his job is *protected* by Ethics, 150
    person in one job position not doing that job, but doing every other –, 139
    person not doing his job becomes the focus of investigation by Ethics, 150
    person who is hatted can control his job position, 9
    positions are stable items, 20
    – takeover, Power Change Formula, 60
    usually, an employee has to know more jobs than his own, 33
    security, 34, 147

what is your –?, 33
when writing a memo, address it to the *JOB POSITION*, 105
you keep your job in a good organization by *doing* your –, 34

Job Endangerment, 152

junior(s),
always require the – to state or initial "This is okay" on all work, actions or projects, 106, 114, 131
as a junior, duplicate the order, and never fail to clarify if you have misunderstood, 138
Danger Formula is the formula an executive applies when he assigns a – a Condition of Danger, 54
issue so many orders unknown to a senior and *across* his lines, 120
never let a – say "is this okay?" 114, 131
problems presented by –, 130
those in charge fail to brief their –, 119
who propose unusual solutions generally don't know the policy or orders anyway, 139

justice,
definition, 146
factor is quite mild (Normal Condition), 57
identifying any justice action or symbol of justice with oppression, 150

K

know-how,
an employee is only limited in what he can do in the organization by lack of –, 33
organizing is the know-how of changing things, 35

knowledge,
and the K-R-C Triangle, 9, 10
definition, 9
is an element of coordination, 101

Knowledge Report(s), 152

KRC (Knowledge, Responsibility, Control)
ignoring the losses and making the wins firm, 11
little by little one can make anything go right, 10
– Triangle functions like the A-R-C Triangle, 10

L

Liability,
battle plan can become a liability, 98-99
Condition, 65
Formula, 66

Liability Formula, *see* **Liability**

lines,
and Power Change, 60
ball-up of –, 125, 126
comm –, 25-28, 33, 132, 140
employees not grooved in on the –, 129
executive seldom hit by catastrophe unless he has had noncompliance on his –, 132
failure to comply with an order can set an emergency flap going which crowds the lines with memos, 116
get that change off the –, 57
if different parts of an organization are not *coordinated*, they begin to cross each other's lines and tangle, 101
juniors issue so many orders unknown to a senior and across his –, 120
keep current work visible and where it belongs on the –, 109
make a record of all your job position's –, 59
memos held up on –, 140
no work that is active may be put in desk drawers or hidden off the –, 108
origination – (Expanded Non-Existence Formula), 53
string –, 29
Suppression On – (Dev-t #8), 120
take unwilling personnel off the lines and traffic busyness drops by two-thirds and effectiveness increases by many times, 115
there is no system of lines on a graph to determine a trend, 79
Using Dev-T As An Excuse To Cut – (Dev-t #34), 132
what an executive wants on his –, 29
what an executive's – should look like, 32

M

Major Target, 121, 122

manage(ment),
coordination is the essence of –, 101
middle –, 98
of a company is at its best when there is a strategic plan, 98

top –, 98
when you manage by the statistic, you don't go wrong, 74

memorandum(s),
and Ethics Report form, 152
CSW is an assembled –, 112
definition, 105
routing –, 105, 106
types of –, 105

misunderstood word,
and study, iii-iv
the most common cause of unacceptable production on the job, 15
understanding ceases on going past a –, 15
vocabularies have to be increased, 16

morale,
definition, 35
good organization equals good –, 35
organization and –, 35
production is the basis of –, 130

N

noncompliance,
a cause of Executive Enturbulence, 132
catastrophes can occur because of –, 117
one consequence of – when repeated over a long period, 117
type of Ethics Report, 152

Non-Existence,
applies when taking over a collapsed position, 62
Condition, 52
description of slant of line on graph, 69
Expanded Non-Existence Formula, 53
Formula, 52
misapplication of –, 52

Non-Existence Formula, *see* **Non-Existence**

Normal Operation,
and Power Change Formula, 60
Condition, 56
description of slant of line on graph, 71
Formula, 57

Normal Formula, *see* **Normal Operation**

O

off-line,
Dev-t #24, 128
people who are *always* –, 34

personally delivering a memo is –, 26
using a phone instead of sending a memo is –, 26

off-origin,
Dev-t #23, 127

off-policy, 152

orders,
and altered compliance, 117
are held by the recipient until completed, 30
backflashes are unnecessary responses to –, 29
Cross Orders (Dev-T #9), 120
enforce extant orders in Power Change, 60
Misunderstood Orders (Dev-T #44), 137
noncompliance with valid –, 152
Present-Time Orders Only (Dev-T #10), 121
query of –, 30, 31
Relaying An Order In A Confusing Manner (Dev-T #45), 138
Staledated Orders (Dev-T #16), 125
Unclear Orders (Dev-T #43), 137

organization(s),
and goodwill, 159
and morale, 35
and the principles of exchange, 41
anything in an organization is your job if it lessens confusion if you do it, 33
as the understanding among coworkers increases, so will the level of cooperation in an –, 1
basic words of –, 15
bound together by common purposes, 101
consists of certain people doing certain jobs, 17
each member of an organization is a specialist, 19
form of the –, 121, 122
good morale is the product of good –, 35
Incorrect – (Dev-T #25), 128
job position not covered throws randomness into the –, 157
misunderstood words of –, iv
one reads the division statistics for the *week*, 69
– operate on statistics, 69
prosperity of a business is directly proportional to the speed of flow of its particles, 159
public knows an organization by its appearance, 160
theory of –, 17
without an org board will break down by overload and cross-flows and crosscurrents, 19

organizational genius, 22

organizing,
is the know-how of changing things, 35

organizing board,
and the theory of organization, 17
as the org board is changed, the Comm Center baskets are changed, 108
definition, 17
duties of an employee, 157
if we only have one person in an organization he would still have to have a sort of –, 19
is a perpetual combination of flows, 22
must also provide for pulling in the materials, disposing of the product and being paid for the cycle of action and its supervision, 21
Org Board Dev-t (Dev-t #26), 129
patterns, 18

out-basket(s), 108

out-ethics,
and Knowledge Reports, 152
and the First Dynamic Danger Formula, 55
defined, 146
when – is occurring in a group, it is almost impossible for other members of the group not to know of it, 151

overburden, 26

P

particle(s),
an organization's positions change flowing –, 20
and confusion, 20
flow *in sequence*, 20
one begins to move out of cope by getting people to handle the types of particles of the organization, 23
one has to be able to see where a particle comes in and where it leaves, 22
one has to be able to spot any point a particle will halt, and mend that part of the flow or handle it, 22
one organizes by surveying the types of –, 21
one organizes by working out the changes desired for each particle along the sequence of changes, 21
prosperity of a business is directly proportional to the speed of flow of its particles, 159
Removing Particles Off The Line (Dev-T #50), 140
with present-time orders only, the particles of the organization eventually become thoroughly entangled, 122
you can create confusion by handling another's particles, *but* you will also discover that you can create confusion by not handling another's particles on occasion, 33

pending basket,
and how to handle work, 141
defined, 108
incomplete CSW causes *pending* basket to overload, 111
items that have been looked at but cannot be dealt with immediately, 141

planning,
below strategic planning one has tactical planning, 97
consists of the setting of all targets of all types, 121
is an element of coordination, 101
strategy is planning done at the level of senior executives, 97

policy(ies),
code of offenses and their penalties should become firm and expressed –, 149
conformation with – (Expanded Non Existence Formula), 53
each employee is responsible for seeing that company policy is carried out, 157
formulate and adopt firm – (1st Dynamic Danger Formula), 55
go out by not being enforced (Dev-t #10, Present-time Orders Only), 121, 122
juniors who propose unusual solutions generally don't know the –, 139
recommend any firm – (Danger Formula), 54
Senior –, 159
study the policies of the company (Power Change Formula), 60
targeting of actions necessary to accomplish quotas should conform to –, 89
unwilling employee always makes dev-t out of every –, 115
when policy exists but is not made known, random policy setting will occur (Dev-t #10, Present-time Orders Only), 121

power,
    in order to discover one's – (K-R-C Triangle), 9
    of an organization is directly proportional to its speed of particle flow, 140

Power,
    as related to Affluence, 59, 83
    Condition for an individual, 59
    Condition, 59
    definition, 59
    description of statistic in –, 59, 83
    even with statistics validly in a Power range, one would handle a dip in the statistics with the appropriate Condition formula, 74
    Formula, 59
    is a *trend*, 59
    is not a one-week thing, 59
    must be determined by more than one week's worth of statistics, 71
    Normal *trend* maintained in a high, high, range, 83
    operating in this new range, slight dip in the stat now and then is still –, 59
    sample graph, 83

Power Change,
    Condition, 60
    Condition not determined by one's own statistic, 52
    Formula, 60
    is actually a person assuming a Condition that has been held from Power by someone else, 60
    one takes over a going concern by the Power Change Formula, 61

Power Change Formula, *see* **Power Change**

Power Formula, *see* **Power**

Present-Time Orders Only (Dev-t #10), 121

Primary Targets,
    a group of "understood" or continuing targets, 121

product(s),
    definition, 39
    don't ever happen by themselves, 40
    hope of a product has a short-term value, 42
    is exchange, 39
    name, want and get your –, 40
    to have a *product*, something must flow OUT, 20

production,
    if it's not occurring, the ability to name the product is probably missing, 40
    is an element of coordination, 101
    is the basis of morale, 130
    slows or stops as a result of incorrect organization (Dev-t #25, Incorrect Organization), 128
    you get nonproduction when you penalize –, 150

Professionalism, 161

program(s),
    a new program should be administered only as a "special project" for a while, 63
    mini –, 98, 101
    tactical planners are simply those people putting strategic plans into programs and projects, 97-98
    targets, 98-99, 121

project(s),
    always require the junior to state or initial "This is okay" on all work, actions or –, 106, 114, 131
    and CSW's, 111, 114
    duty of the Inspections Officer is to inspect the status of various –, 147
    Having To Have Before They Can Do (Dev-t #30) causes projects to stall, 130
    how to get approval of actions and –, 111
    Liability Condition is assigned where careless or malicious and knowing damage is caused to –, 65
    new program should be administered only as a "special project" for a while, 63
    Removing Particles Off The Line (Dev-t #50) can sabotage –, 140
    tactical planners are simply those people putting strategic plans into programs and –, 97-98
    when one can not make up one's mind as to…a project…, a Condition of Doubt exists, 66

PR, (Public Relations),
    excellent technical delivery is what generates a blaze of goodwill and –, 159
    PRing, 41

Q

quality,
    goodwill and high – delivery, 159
    how well organized things are *improves* –, 41
    lack of viability can always be traced to the volume and quality of an actual valuable final product, 41
    person who is filled with the quality of affinity will automatically find people anywhere near him also beginning to be filled with affinity, 1
    produce in abundance and try to give better than expected –, 47
    producing in VOLUME or –, 41
    product and –, 41

quantity,
    a *graph* is a line or diagram showing how one quantity depends on, compares with or changes another, 84
    statistics refer to the quantity of work done, 51

quota(s),
    and sample subproduct list, 88
    any quota can be targeted for increase daily and weekly, 88
    by monitoring daily graphs, new quotas can be projected, 92
    by setting quotas and establishing targets that will achieve the quotas, an executive can get his statistics rising, 93
    can be and should be set for subproducts, 87
    definition, 87
    established should be real and always higher than those of the week before, 88
    setting –, 87, 88
    targeting of actions necessary to accomplish quotas are definite, should conform to company policy, and be *doable*, 89
    targeting of statistics and –, 87

R

rationalizing
    statistics, 74

reality,
    affinity and reality are very much less important than communication, 6
    and the ARC Triangle, 6
    and the physical universe, 2
    component of Understanding, 1
    definition, 1
    if the organizing board does not reflect the reality of your job title(s), 158
    is agreement, 1
    quickest way to drive someone insane is to do something to his –, 2

reasonable(ness),
    all this is being – (Rationalizing Statistics), 74
    an employee or executive can be "reasonable" and accept reasons why something cannot be done, 135
    if a moral code were thoroughly –, 146
    justice factor is quite mild and quite – (Normal Condition Formula), 57
    Reasonableness (Dev-T #39), 135
    when you are being reasonable, you don't catch the improvements or flubs that, piled up, wreck an organization, 74

refer(s)(al)(ring)
    Failure To Complete A Cycle of Action, And Referral (Dev-t #41), 136
    Hat Dumping is referring everything to someone else (Dev-t #19), 126
    people to the correct terminal, 157
    the way to get rid of traffic is to do it, not to refer it, 141
    what you should specialize in is terminating a situation, not referring it to someone else, 136

report(s)(ing)
    embroidered –, 31
    Ethics Reports, 151
    False Reports (Dev-T #1), 116
    Inspections and Reports, 147
    No Reports (Dev-T #4), 117
    only by writing Ethics Reports can bad spots in the company be recognized and corrected, 154
    sample Ethics Report, 153
    Things That Shouldn't Be Report, 153

responsibility,
    and the K-R-C Triangle, 9
    definition, 9
    executives have varying degrees of financial –, 32
    for actions (CSW), 114
    for your job is very low (Developed Traffic), 115
    it is folly to try to control something or even know something without –, 10
    Lack Of Executive Responsibility (Dev-T #32), 131

should be clearly distinguished from *blame* or *praise*, 9

reward(s),
    and penalties, 149
    are not necessarily proportional to one's contribution, 149
    if you reward nonproduction you get nonproduction, 150
    inequalities of workload, rewards unearned, no havingness — these are some of the things that are snarled about, 35
    is what one desires, not what is given, 149
    when work no longer has reward, none will work, 150
    when you reward down-statistics and penalize up-statistics you get down-statistics, 150

route(s)(ing)(ed),
    by channels, 152, 153
    comm line is the route along which communication travels, 25
    org board and –, 17
    original Ethics Report is routed to the Ethics Officer, 152
    up from apathy or inaction, 10

S

scale,
    correctly scaled graph, example, 86
    correct scaling is the essence of good graphing, 86
    definition, 84
    graph line changes, too large or too small, result, 84
    horizontal –, 84
    how to figure the –, 84
    incorrectly scaled graph, example, 85
    need not figure scale for more than one graph at a time, 84
    of Conditions, 51
    plotting a graph "upside down" so far as the numerical vertical scale on the left is concerned, 72
    vertical –, 84

section,
    and the principles of exchange, 41
    in-charge, 88
    reads its statistics by the *hour*, 69
    there are two sections within I&R, Inspections and Ethics, 147
    whole theory of successful organization is to have sections that specialize, 17

senior(s),
    assigning junior a Danger Condition, 54
    Completed Staff Work and –, 111
    executive, 32, 54, 97, 98, 102
    fail to brief their juniors (Info Failure, Dev-T #6), 119
    forwarding large quantities of irrelevant information to a – (Dev-t #38), 134
    Job Endangerment Report is normally written on a –, 152
    junior asks his senior, "Is this okay?" (Dev-t #32), 131
    juniors fail to inform seniors of data they have (Info Failure, Dev-T #6), 119
    juniors issue so many orders unknown to a senior and *across* his lines (Dev-T #9), 120
    Lack of CSW (Dev-T #7) and –, 119
    major appointments and dismissals of key personnel must be okayed by a senior executive before the fact, 32
    orders and directives travel from senior to junior, 25
    solving problems presented by juniors (Dev-t #29), 130

senior policy, 159

service(s)
    and exchange in abundance, 46
    and partial exchange, 45
    and product, 39, 40
    dev-t costs a company the – of two-thirds of its personnel, 115
    goodwill and –, 159, 160
    must be as close to instant as possible, 159
    public expects good –, 159
    quality of –, 159
    smart, friendly service versus sloppy, "help yourself" –, 160
    speed of –, 159

service facilities, 58

speed
    and service facilities, 176
    CSW's are employed to increase speed of action, 111
    of information to an executive, 32
    of particle flow, 140, 159
    of service, 159

stable terminal, 20

staff meetings,
    each person in the group is responsible for…, 102

purpose of –, 101
topics routinely covered in –, 102

statistic(s),
closer one is to the scene of a statistic, the smaller amount of time per statistic is needed to interpret it, 76
Conditions from Non-Existence through Power are declared on the basis of –, 51
correct scaling, 84
daily graphs, 91
definition, 51
discount a fall just because stats are high, high, high is folly, 74
down –, 74, 150
each employee must keep a daily graph of his –. 91
ethics actions are often used to handle down-statistics, 150
every job should have an assigned statistic that represents its work or production, 87
how to correctly determine the trend, 78-79
how to figure the scale, 84
how to read them, 69
how to read trends, 78
incorrect figuring of scale, 84
interpretation of trend, 76
judgment and –, 74
nagging around about a rise in –, 74
one applies the Condition of Emergency when statistics are seen to be *declining* or are *unchanging*, 55
one applies the First Dynamic Danger Formula when his personal statistic is in a Danger Condition, 55
only sound measure of any production or any job or any activity, 51
penalize down-statistics only, 150
promote by statistic only, 150
rationalization of –, 74
reading –, 69
trend(s), *see* **trend(s)**
upside down graphs, 72
up –, 150
what they measure, 51
when you have a line going steeply up on a statistic graph, that's Affluence, 57
when you reward down-statistics and penalize up-statistics, you get down-statistics, 150

strategic plan(ning),
and top management, 98
defined, 97

subproduct(s),
a valid subproduct list will greatly increase organization efficiency and show up holes, 43
compiling a list of –, 41
quotas can be and should be set for –, 87
relationship to VFPs, 42
sample subproducts list, 42
test of any subproduct list, 43

T

tactical plan(ning),
and middle management, 98
below strategic planning one has –, 97
must integrate into the strategic plan and accomplish the strategic plan, 97
tells exactly who to move what to where and exactly what to do at that point, 97

target(s)(ed),
any quota can be targeted for increase daily or weekly, 88
battle plan is defined as a written list of doable –, 97
Bugged Targets (Dev-t #14), 123
by monitoring daily graphs, targets can be unbugged, new targets can be established, 92
by setting quotas and establishing targets that will achieve the quotas, an executive can get his statistics rising, 93
can be unbugged, 92
Cross Targets (Dev-t #13), 123
definition, 88
Major –, 121, 122
Primary –, 121
program –, 121
two types of –, 121
Unreal Targets (Dev-t #12), 122-123

targeting,
definition, 88
do not permit nebulous generalities to occur on the targeting cycle of action, 89
Nonexistent Targeting (Dev-t #11), 122
of statistics and quotas, 87
understanding and competent use of targeting in battle plans is vital to overall accomplishment, 99

technology,
Hubbard Administrative –, xi
of HANDLING things, 10
to graphing stats, 72

terminal(s),
 make yourself known to every – (Expanded Non-Existence Condition Formula), 53
 not necessary to have a stable terminal do only one thing, 20
 one *organizes* by posting the –, 21
 refer people to the correct –, 157
 with present-time orders only, the terminals, lines and particles eventually become thoroughly entangled, 122

Things That Shouldn't Be, 153

"This is okay", 106, 114, 131

three-basket system, 108

trend(s),
 are not hard to read, but it is done with the EYE, 79
 can be anything from Danger to Power, 78
 definition, 76
 example, Affluence –, 83
 example, Danger –, 81
 example, Emergency –, 81, 82
 example, Non-Existence –, 80
 example, Normal –, 82
 example, Power –, 83
 it is also possible to have a Non-Existence trend, 78
 more remote governing body would interpret stats using a –, 78
 Power is a –, 59, 83
 presentation of stats and trends in staff meeting, 102
 reading stat –, 78
 to determine a statistic trend one needs to look at several weeks' worth of statistics, 76
 used to estimate expansion or warn of contraction, 76
 visually averaging the peaks and valleys to determine –, 78

U

Understanding,
 and the definition of the Communication Formula, 118
 as it increases among coworkers, so will the level of cooperation, 1
 ceases on going past a misunderstood word or concept, 15
 components of –, 1

upside down graphs, 72

up-statistic(s), *see* **statistics**

V

valuable final product,
 and subproduct lists, 42
 could as easily be named a VALUABLE EXCHANGEABLE PRODUCT, 41
 definition, 41
 is *valuable* because it is potentially or factually exchangeable, 41
 there and being exchanged determines basic survival, 41

viability,
 how well things are organized *increases* production volume and *improves* quality and thus can bring about viability, 41
 lack of viability can always be traced to the volume and quality of an actual valuable final product, 41

W

Work,
 how to handle –, 141